# STONEHENGE

A

# TEMPLE

RESTOR'D

TO THE

## British Druids.

---

By *WILLIAM STUKELEY*, M. D.

Rector of *All Saints* in STAMFORD.

---

−*Deus est qui non mutatur in ævo.*     MANILIUS.

=========================================

*LONDON:*

Printed for W. INNYS and R. MANBY, at the West End of
St. *Paul's.*

MDCCXL.

[1740]

Stonehenge: A Temple Restored
to the British Druids
by William Stukeley, M. D.

A Cornerstone Book
Published by Cornerstone Book Publishers
An Imprint of Michael Poll Publishing
Copyright © 2009 by Cornerstone Book Publishers

Cornerstone Book Publishers
New Orleans, LA

First Cornerstone Edition - 2009

www.cornerstonepublishers.com

ISBN: 1-934935-45-X
ISBN 13: 978-1-934935-45-3

MADE IN THE USA

# STONEHENGE

A

# TEMPLE

## RESTOR'D

### TO THE

# 𝔅𝔯𝔦𝔱𝔦𝔰𝔥 𝔇𝔯𝔲𝔦𝔡𝔰.

By *WILLIAM STUKELEY*, M. D.
Rector of *All Saints* in STAMFORD.

――*Deus est qui non mutatur in ævo.*      MANILIUS.

*LONDON:*

Printed for W. INNYS and R. MANBY, at the West End
of St. *Paul's.*

MDCCXL.

To His GRACE

# PEREGRINE

Duke of Ancaster and Kesteven,

Hereditary Lord Great Chamberlain of

ENGLAND, *&c. &c.*

*May it please your* GRACE,

TO accept of this attempt to illustrate one of the noblest antiquities now left upon earth. I am confident your Grace will not dislike it, either because it is a religious antiquity, or because it belongs to our own country.

Your Grace best shews your regard to religion, by a constant attendance on its duties, in the service of the church; and by a regular practice of its precepts, in their whole extent. And as you are justly sensible, the foundation of religion rests on a careful observance of the sabbath: you not only study to encourage it, by your own great example; but likewise discountenance, that too fashionable custom of travelling on sundays, and other profanations thereof: which are the sure root of national corruption, the sure presage of national ruin.

Nor are your Grace's virtues more conspicuous, in your religious and moral character, than in the love of your country. This you inherit with the blood that runs in your veins; this you derive from an immemorial series of noble ancestors, renowned in our annals, for their ready allegiance to the sovereign power; for their vigor in support of the constitution both in church and state; that have often hazarded and ruined their fortunes, and poured out their blood, in its defence. I might instance particularly, the great part they bore in the Reformation, the Restoration and the Revolution.

After the honour I have enjoyed of having been long known to your Grace: I could enlarge upon the amiable qualities of your private life, your domestic and social virtues, your humane and beneficent disposition to all around you, friends or dependants, or those of your own family. With truth I might say, that you never refused to serve any person that applied to you, where it was in your power: that you never knowingly did an unkind, an injurious thing to any person: that no one ever withdrew griev'd from your presence. I can safely affirm, and fear no contradiction, that justice, honour and honesty are some of the real jewels, that adorn your Grace's coronet. And they, at this time of day, receive a seasonable lustre, from your high nation, and illustrious birth.

But the agreeableness of the subject insensibly drew me from my main purpose, which was to make this publick acknowledgment, of the great favours your Grace has confer'd upon me: and to beg leave to profess myself,

> *May it please your* GRACE,
> *Your* GRACE'S *most humble,*
> *And most devoted servant,*
> *Jan.* 1. 1739-40.
> William Stukeley

# PREFACE.

A few years ago I spent some time every summer in viewing, measuring, and considering the works of the ancient Druids in our Island; I mean; I mean those remarkable circles of Stones which we find all over the kingdom, many of which I have seen, but of many more I have had accounts. Their greatness and number astonish'd me, nor need I be afraid to say, their beauty and design, as well as antiquity, drew my particular attention. I could not help carrying my inquiries about them as far as I was able. My studies this way have produc'd a vast quantity of drawings and writing, which consider'd as an intire work, may thus be intitled,

## Patriarchal CHRISTIANITY:

OR,

## A Chronological HISTORY

OF THE

**Origin and Progress of true Religion, and of Idolatry.**

*The parts of which the whole is compos'd are these:*

I. Canon Mosaicæ Chronologiæ, *or the year of* Moses *settled, by which he reckons time in the history of the old world; the time of the year fix'd when creation was begun. This is done in a new manner, and becomes an intire system of chronology from the creation to the* Exodus, *and is exemplified by many particular Kalendars of the most remarkable transactions; which are proofs of the truth of the Canon. There are interspersed a great many astronomical and historical illustrations of the sacred pages, particu-*

*larly* Sanchoniathon's *genealogies, and* Manethon's Egyptian Dynasties, *are applied in a new Method to the history and chronology of the Scriptures.*

II. Melchisedec, *or a delineation of the first and patriarchal religion, from the best light we can gather in the sacred history; and from the most ancient heathen customs, which were remains of that religion. In this Treatise it is shewn, that the first religion was no other than Christianity, the Mosaic dispensation, as a veil, intervening; that all mankind from the creation had a knowledge of the plurality of persons in the Deity.*

III. *Of the mysteries of the ancients, one of the first deviations from true religion, to idolatry; this is chiefly pursu'd in an explication of the famous table of* Isis, *or* Bembin-table, *publish'd by* Pignorius, Kircher, *&c. wherein that knowledge which the ancients had concerning the true nature of the Deity, is further explain'd.*

IV. *A discourse on the hieroglyphic learning of the ancients, and of the origin of the alphabet of letters. Very many hieroglyphic monuments of the* Egyptians *are explain'd, more especially those that relate to their true notions of the persons in the Deity. The time and rise of the alphabet of letters is deduc'd from a new foundation. The present square* Hebrew *characters are shewn to be the primitive idea of letters, from whence all others are deriv'd. Whence the idea of every letter was taken? an explanation of all the old* Hebrew *coins with* Samaritan *characters.*

V. *The patriarchal history, particularly of* Abraham, *is largely pursu'd; and the deduction of the* Phœnician *colony into the Island of* Britain, *about or soon after his time; whence the origin of the* Druids, *of their Religion and writing; they brought the patriarchal Religion along with them, and same knowledge of symbols or hieroglyphics, like those of the ancient* Egyptians; *they had the*

7

*notion and expectation of the Messiah, and of the time of the year when he was to be born, of his office and death.*

VI. *Of the Temples of the Druids in Britain, their religious rites, orders, sacrifices, groves, tombs, their* cursus's, *places of forts and exercises, &c. particularly an ample and accurate description of that stupendous temple of theirs at* Abury *in* North Wiltshire, *the most august work at this day upon the globe of the earth; with many prints of ground plots, views and admeasurements of all its parts; of their manner of sepulture; an account of my digging into many of their barrows and* tumuli, *with drawings of them, &c.*

VII. *Of the celebrated* Stonehenge, *another Temple of theirs, with prints of that work; an account of the barrows I dug up, and what was discover'd in then; of the knowledge the Druids had of the magnetical compass, and conjectures of the particular times when these works were made, long before Cæsar arriv'd in* Britain.

*I propose to publish these two first, and proceed to the speculative parts afterwards; reserving them, God willing, to the maturer time of my life.*

*My intent is (besides preserving the memory of these extraordinary monuments, so much to the honour of our country, now in great danger of ruin) to promote, as much as I am able, the knowledge and practice of ancient and true Religion; to revive in the minds of the learned the spirit of Christianity, nearly as old as the Creation, which is now languishing among us; to restore the first and great Idea of the Deity, who has carry'd on the same regular and golden chain of Religion from the beginning to this day; to warm our hearts into that true sense of Religion, which keeps the medium between ignorant superstition and learned free-thinking, between slovenly fanaticism and popish pageantry, between enthusiasm and the rational worship of God, which is no where upon earth done, in my judgment, better than in the Church of* England. *And feeing a spirit of Scepticism has of late become so fashionable and audacious as to strike at the fundamentals of all revelation, I have endeavoured to trace it back to the fountain of Divinity, whence it flows; and shew that Religion is one system as old as the world, and that is the Christian Religion; that God did not leave the rational part of his creation, like the colony of an ant-hill, with no other guide than instinct, but proportion'd his discoveries to the age of the world, to the learning, wisdom, and experience of it; as a wise parent does now to his children. I shall shew likewise, that our predecessors, the Druids of* Britain, *tho' left in the extremest west to the improvement of their own thoughts, yet advanc'd their inquiries, under all disadvantages, to such heights, as should make our moderns asham'd, to wink in the sunshine of learning and religion. And we may with reason conclude, there was somewhat very extraordinary in those principles, which prompted them to such a noble spirit as produced these works, still visible with us, which for grandeur, simplicity and antiquity, exceed any of the* European *wonders.*

*That the doctrines and works of the Druids have hitherto been so little considered (since authors only transcribe from one to another, the few remaining scraps to be found in classic writers) was an incentive to me likewise in the following attempt, and at the same time it pleads for me, and bespeaks the reader's favour. I want likewise the great advantages to be had from a knowledge of the remaining* Celtic *languages, books, manuscripts, and history, the* Cornish, Welsh, Irish, Highland, *&c. the chief repository now of their doctrines and customs; so that in my own opinion I may very well say with the poet,*

Interea Dryadum silvas & saxa sequamur
Intactas, tua Mecænas haud mollia jussa.   *Virgil.*

*And tho' there has been of late a large volume publish'd on the subject of Stonehenge, yet we may well say there has nothing been wrote upon the subject. Nor have I any other notion of this performance, than that it is as a first attempt to say something upon*

9

*those famous philosophers and priests the Druids, who are never spoken of in antiquity but with a note of admiration; and are always rank'd with the Magi of the Persians, the gymnosophists of the Indians, the prophets and hierophants of the Egyptians, and those sort of patriarchal priests, whose orders commenc'd before idolatry began; from whom the Pythagoreans, Platonists, and Greek philosophers learn'd the best things they knew. To clear away rubbish, and lay a foundation only, in this difficult and obscure work, is doing somewhat. The method of writing which I have chose is a diffusive one, not pretending to a formal and stiff scholastic proof of every thing I say, which would be odious and irksome to the reader, as well as myself. The knowledge I have acquired in these matters, was from examining and studying their works; the proofs are deriv'd from distant and different topicks, and it would be very inconvenient to marshal them syllogistically in a work of this nature; the proof results from the intire work; in all matters of so great antiquity it must be found out by the reader; and to one that has proper sagacity and judgment, conviction will steal upon him insensibly, if I am not mistaken; and he will own the evidence in general, is as strong as the nature of the subject will bear, or requires.*

*It was very disagreeable to me that I was forc'd to combat against a book publish'd in the name of the celebrated Inigo Jones, for whose memory I have the greatest regard. I wonder the publisher of that work did not think of a very easy method to convince himself that he was in an error. If Stonehenge is a Roman work, it was certainly built by the Roman scale; had he reduc'd his own measures to that standard, he would have seen the absurdity of his opinion; for we cannot think that a temple, or elegant building, as he would have it, should not shew its founders by the scale on which it is form'd; they are all fractions in the Roman scale, undoubted evidence that the Romans had no hand in it. For there is no meaning, no design in the choice of the measures, neither in general nor particular; a thing unworthy of a great architect, or a great design. But it appears very evident to me, that Inigo Jones had little or no part in that work, especially as it is moulded at present; and I think I have reason to be of opinion that he never drew the designs therein published, because I should be unwilling to say he knowingly falsified them. I have very much shortened what I had to say against that book, because I have no love for wrangling, and barely mention'd what was necessary, that the reader may have a true notion of this noble antiquity.*

Plate 1: A Druid

# STONEHENGE

## A WORK of the

## 𝔅𝔯𝔦𝔱𝔦𝔰𝔥 𝔇𝔯𝔲𝔦𝔡𝔰

### DESCRIB'D.

## CHAP. I.

*Of the Situation of* Stonehenge *in general. That it was a temple of the Druids, of the patriarchal mode, who were a most ancient oriental colony. In later times, the* Belgæ *from the continent, conquer'd this country from them. Whence these stones were brought? Of their nature, magnitude, weight. Of the measure of the Druids, the ancient* Hebrew *cubit, and its proportion to the* English *foot.*

THE *Wiltshire* downs, or *Salisbury* plain, (as commonly call'd) for extent and beauty, is, without controversy, one of the most delightful parts of *Britain*. But of late years great encroachments have been made upon it by the plough, which threatens the ruin of this fine champain, and of all the monuments of antiquity thereabouts. Monuments, we can scarce say, whether more wonderful in themselves, more observ'd, or less understood! among them, *Stonehenge* has been eminent from the remotest ages, tho' 'tis not the greatest, most considerable, or most ancient. But 'tis my intent to begin my discourse from it, because the latest, and from thence proceed upwards in our inquiries, about the times and au-

13

thors of these stupendous works, the temples of the Druids in our Island: for I cannot doubt that *Stonehenge* was such. The idea we conceive of the distance of time, when these kind of works were made, cannot be ill-form'd, if we consider, that the utmost accounts of 'em we have in writing, are from the *Britons*, the remains of the people who lived here, at the time of the *Roman* invasion. This is mention'd in some manuscripts of *Ninnius* before the *Saxons* and *Danes* came over. And the oldest *Britons* speak of this only by tradition, far above all memorial. They wonder'd at *Stonehenge* then, and were as far to seek about the founders and intent of it, as we now. They have recourse to magic, as is usual, when they would account for any thing seemingly so much above human power, to accomplish. They tell us, these stones of immense bulk were brought from a plain, in the middle of *Ireland*, and the like. Which reports give us only no obscure hint of their true authors, the Druids, who were fam'd for magic, and were driven last into *Ireland*, in the time of the *Romans*. There they built such like works again, or their brethren had built before; till Christianity, to which the greatest and purest part of their own doctrine was akin, soon put TAB. I. an end to their polity, which the *Roman* arms could not do. And they embrac'd that religion, to which their own opinions and rites had so direct a tendency. This is the sentiment of *Origen* on *Ezekiel* iv. And 'tis sufficiently evident, if we consider, that the first planters of Christianity in *Ireland*, immediately converted the whole island, without so much as the blood of one martyr. Nay, the Druids themselves, at that time the only national priests, embraced it readily, and some of them were very zealous preachers of it, and effectual converters of others. For instance, the great *Columbanus* himself was a Druid: the apostle of *Ireland*, *Cornwall*, &c. We need not be surpriz'd at this, when we assert, that there is very much reason to believe, these famous philosophic priests came hither, as a *Phœnician* colony, in the very earliest times, even as soon as *Tyre* was founded: during the life of the patriarch *Abraham*, or very soon after. Therefore they brought along with them the patriarchal religion, which was so extremely like Christianity, that in effect it differ'd from it only in this; they believed in a Messiah who was to come into the world, as we believe in him that is come. Further, they came from that very country where *Abraham* liv'd, his sons and grandsons; a family God almighty had separated from the gross of mankind, to stifle the seeds of idolatry; a mighty prince, and preacher of righteousness. And tho' the memoirs of our Druids are extremely short, yet we can very evidently discover from them, that the Druids were of *Abraham's* religion intirely, at least in the earliest times, and worshipp'd the supreme Being in the same manner as he did, and probably according to his example, or the example of his and their common ancestors.

All this I shall prove, in the pursuit of this work. But before we come to speculation, intend to give an exact description of their several temples, and the like works; for such will be a good foundation for us to build upon. That we may proceed from things evident and more known, to those less known, and which we design to make evident, as well as we are able, and the nature of it will permit. A matter so immers'd in the dark mist of time, where very few scatter'd traces remain, must needs bespeak the reader's candor. The dignity of the subject will excuse my boldness in attempting one so difficult. And however I succeed in accounting for these wonderful works; at least, I shall be instrumental in preserving their memory, in giving just drawings of them.

*Stonehenge*, by the extravagant grandeur of the work, has attracted the eyes and admiration of all ages. After the reformation, upon the revival of learning among us, the curious began to consider it more intimately, I cannot say successfully. Mr. *Camden* rose as the sun of antiquity, that put out former lights, and, like *Cæsar*, affrights all that value a reputation, from attempting any thing in his way. His great skill in *Roman* learning, and our *English* history, only enabled him to be, as it were, silent on *Stonehenge*. He saw with excellent judgment, that neither *Roman* nor *English* had place there, or could serve to illustrate it. He writes modestly, as his manner was; "Of these things I am not able so much to give an accurate account, as mightily to grieve, that the founders of this noble monument cannot be trac'd out." He could not persuade himself that either *Romans*, *Saxons* or *Danes* had any hand in it. And as for his representation of it in picture, I verily believe, it was drawn only from fancy or memory, or by some engraver from his oral description. *A.D.* 1620, king *James* I. being at the earl of *Pembroke's* seat at *Wilton*, and agreeably surpriz'd with the sight of *Stonehenge*, consulted the famous architect *Inigo Jones*, upon it; thinking it a matter in his way. This great man, who deservedly may be stiled the *English Vitruvius*, gave his opinion of it, as a *Roman* work; and left, I suppose, some few indigested notes in writing thereupon.

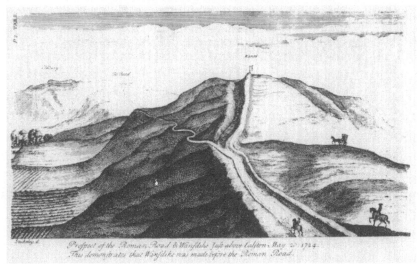

Plate 2. Prospect of the Roman Road and Wansdike Just above Calston, May 20, 1724. This demonstrates that Wansdike was made before the Roman Road.

From which his son-in-law *John Webb* compos'd an intire treatise, endeavouring to prove it. But they that are acquainted with *Roman* architecture, or have consider'd *Stonehenge*, must needs be of a different opinion. And as my Lord Bishop of *London* well observes, in his notes on *Camden*, "it cannot be safe to close with Mr. *Jones*, tho' his book otherwise be a learned and ingenious piece." *Inigo Jones* lived 30 years after this, and yet Mr. *Webb* makes an apology for his work, "that if he had surviv'd to have done it, with his own and, it would have been better." But 'tis very reasonably believ'd, that tho' *Inigo Jones* was an extraordinary genius in architecture, yet he wanted many qualifications for an author, especially in such a work as *Stonehenge*. 'Tis my opinion, that had his architectonic skill been united to Mr. Camden's learning, he could never have demonstrated *Stonehenge* to be a *Roman* work. Afterwards, Dr. *Charlton* publish'd a piece against *Webb's* performance, and certainly has said enough to overthrow it, tho' he could not with equal success establish his own opinion, that it was the work of the *Danes*. Whereas *Olaus Wormius* finds no such monuments among

17

the *Gothic* nations: which, as Mr. *Toland* observes, is answer sufficient to his allegation. *Webb* answer'd the Doctor's book, and by turns effectually demolish'd his opinion, but could not still vindicate his own. Yet from all their disputations, no spark was struck, towards a discovery of the real truth. What is the worst part in both performances of Mr. *Webb*, his representation of the real monument in his drawings, is fictitious. And, as Mr. *Aubry* rightly observes, "in endeavouring to retrieve a piece of architecture in *Vitruvius*, he abuses the reader with a false representation of the whole." It requires no great pains to prove this, nor need we take much time to be satisfy'd in it: the work is still extant. As soon as a judicious eye comes upon the spot, we discern that *Webb's* equilateral triangles forming the cell are fancies: his three entrances across the ditch are so too; and that he has turn'd the cell a sixth part from its true situation, to savour his imaginary hypothesis. But 'tis against my inclination to find fault with the labours of others, nor do I thereby seek to bribe the reader in my own favour. I had a great pleasure for several years together, in viewing and examining these noble remains of our ancestors. What I wrote about them, was for my private amusement, and that of friends. And I publish them only for the honour of my country, and in hopes that such a publication will not be unserviceable to religion; which is my ultimate view.

Tho' *Stonehenge* be the proudest singularity of this sort, in the world, as far as we know: yet there are so many others, manifestly form'd upon the same, or kindred design, by the same measure, and for the same purpose, all over the *Britanic* isles; that we can have no room to doubt of their being made by the same people, and that by direction of the *British* Druids. There are innumerable, from the land's end in *Cornwall*, to the utmost northern promontory in *Scotland*, where the *Roman* power never reach'd. They are to be found in all the islands between *Scotland* and *Ireland*, isle of *Man*, all the *Orkney* islands, &c. and numerous in *Ireland* itself. And there is no pretence, as far as I can see, for any other persons or nations being the founders of them. They are circles of stones, generally rude, of different diameters, upon elevated ground, barren, open heaths and downs; chiefly made of stones taken from the surface of the ground. There are no remembrances of the founders, any other than an uninter-rupted tradition of their being sacred; that there is medicinal virtue in them; that they were made by the *Irish*; that they were brought from *Afric*; that they were high-places of wor-ship; sanctuaries; bowing, adoring places; and what names they commonly have, intimate the same thing. And in many places the express remembrance and name of Druids re-main, and the people bury their dead in or near them to this day, thinking them holy ground. Mr. *Toland* in his history of the Druids, p. 23. tells us, "In *Gealcossa's* mount in *Inifoen* in the county of *Dunegal*, a Druidess of that name lived; it signi-fies white-legg'd, according to the ancient manner in *Homer's* time. On that hill is her grave and her temple, being a sort of diminutive *Stonehenge*, which the old *Irish*, at this day, dare not any way profane." Many instances of this sort, of all these particulars, we have in our island: particularly the temple on *Temple-downs* by *Abury*. Whatever is dug up in or near these works are manifestly remains of the Druid times; urns, bones, ornaments of amber, glass beads, snake-stones, amulets, celts, flint-hatchets, arrow-heads, and such things as bespeak the rudest ages, the utmost antiquity, most early plantations of people that came into our island, soon after *Noah's* flood. I have all the reason in the world to be-lieve them an oriental colony of *Phœnicians*; at least that such a one came upon the first *Celtic* plantation of people here: which reasons will appear in the progress of this discourse. I suppose in matters of such extraordinary antiquity, it would be absurd to set about a formal demonstration; and those readers would be altogether unreasonable, that expect we prove every fact here, as they would do by living witnesses, before a court of judicature. When all is consider'd, that I have put together on this affair, a judicious person, I presume, will agree, I have made the matter sufficiently evident, and as much as the nature of things requires.

In the times just preceding the coming of the *Romans* into *Britain*, the *Belgæ*, a most powerful colony from the Gallic continent, had firmly seated themselves all over the country, where *Stonehenge* is situate, quite to the southern sea; taking in the south part of *Wiltshire*, and all *Dorsetshire*. *Wiltshire* has its name from the river *Willy*, which in *Welsh* is *wyli*, in *Latin*, *vagire*, from its noise. A river of like name in *Northamptonshire*. Upon the former river at *Wilton*, probably liv'd the *Carvilius*, one of the four kings that fought *Julius Cæsar*, the picture of whole *tumulus* we have given towards the end. The *Belgæ* came into *Britain* upon the south, as other *Celtic* nations before had fix'd themselves from the east, *Kent*, the *Thames*, *&c.* such as the *Cantii, Segontiaci, Atrebates, &c.* so that in *Cæsar*'s time, all the south and east parts of *Britain* were dispossess'd of their original inhabitants, and peopled from the continent: and this very work of *Stonehenge* was in the hands of the *Belgæ*, who built it not. In my *itinerarium curiosum*, p. 181. I observ'd no less than four successive boundary ditches here, from the southern shore; which with good reason, I suppos'd, were made by the *Belgæ*, as they conquer'd the country by degrees, from the aboriginal inhabitants. This shews, they must have been a long while about it, that the *Britons* disputed every inch of ground with them, and that for two reasons; as well because of the extraordinary beauty and goodness of the country, as fighting *pro aris & focis* for their great temple of *Stonehenge:* not to speak of that other greater temple, a little more northward, at *Abury*. The *Segontiaci* had got *Hampshire*, to the east of them, before, as far as the *Colinburn* river, and the *Atrebates, Berkshire.* The first ditch runs between the river of *Blandford,* formerly *Alauna,* and the river of *Bere,* the piddle in *Dorsetshire,* two or three miles south of it. The second runs to the north of *Cranborn* chase, upon the edge of *Wiltshire,* by *Pentridg:* it divides the counties of *Dorset* and *Wilts.* The third is conspicuous upon *Salisbury* plain, as we pass from *Wilton* to *Stonehenge,* about the two-mile stone, north of *Wilton:* it is drawn between the river *Avon* and the *Willy,* from *Dornford* to *Newton.* The fourth is the more famous *Wansdike,* of great extent. *Gwahan* in old *British* signifies *separatio, distinctio* guahanu *seperare,* and that undoubtedly gave name to the ditch. The method of all these ditches, is, to take the northern edge of a ridge of hills, which is always steep; the bank is on the south side. And in my itinerary, p. 134. I show'd a most evident demonstration, that it was made before the time of the *Romans,* in the passage of the *Roman* road down *Runway* hill. TAB. II. *Wansdike* is the last advanc'd post of the *Belgæ* northwards, and that it was

Plate 3. Prospect of Stonehenge from the East by Vespasians camp

made after *Stonehenge* was built, is plain, because the stones that compose the work, were brought from *Marlborough* downs in north *Wiltshire,* beyond the dike; and as then in an enemy's country. And most probably it was built before the *Belgæ* set footing in *Britain,* because of the great number of barrows or sepulchral *tumuli* about it, which, no doubt, were made for the burial of kings and great men.

The stones of which *Stonehenge* is compos'd, beyond any controversy, came from those called the gray weathers, upon *Marlborough* downs near *Abury*; where is that other most wonderful work of this sort, which I shall describe in my next volume. This is 15 or 16 miles off. All the greater stones are of that sort, except the altar, which is of a still harder, as design'd to resist fire. The pyramidals likewise are of a different sort, and much harder than the rest, like those of that other Druid temple call'd *the Weddings*, at *Stanton-drew* in *Somersetshire*. Dr. *Halley* was at *Stonehenge* in the year 1720, and brought a piece of it to the Royal Society. I examin'd it with a microscope. 'Tis a composition of crystals of red, green and white colours, cemented together by nature's art, with opake granules of flinty or stony matter. The Doctor observ'd from the general wear of the weather upon the stones, that the work must be of an extraordinary antiquity, and for ought he knew, 2 or 3000 years old. But had the Doctor been at *Abury*, which is made of the same stones, he might well from the like argumentation conclude, that work as old again as Stonehenge, at least much older, and I verily believe it. Nevertheless the current of so many ages has been more merciful to *Stonehenge*, than the insolence of rapacious hands, (besides the general saccage brought upon the work of old) by the unaccountable folly of mankind, in breaking pieces off with great hammers. This detestable practice arose from the silly notion of the stones being factitious. But, alas! it would be a greater wonder to make them by art, than to carry them 16 miles by art and strength; and those people must be inexcusable, that deface the monument for so trifling a fancy. Another argument of vulgar incogitancy, is, that all the wonder of the work consists, in the difficulty of counting the stones; and with that, the infinite numbers of daily visitants busy themselves. This seems to be the remains of superstition, and the notion of magic, not yet got out of peoples heads, since Druid-times. But indeed a serious view of this magnificent wonder, is apt to put a thinking and judicious person into a kind of ecstacy, when he views the struggle between art and nature, the grandeur of that art that hides itself, and seems unartful. For tho' the contrivance that put this massy frame together, must have been exquisite, yet the founders endeavour'd to hide it, by the seeming rudeness of the work. The bulk of the constituent parts is so very great, that the mortaises and tenons must have been prepar'd to an extreme nicety, and, like the fabric of *Solomon's* temple, every stone tally'd; and neither axes nor hammers were heard upon the whole structure. Nevertheless there is not a stone at *Stonehenge*, that felt not, more or less, both ax and hammer of the founders. Yet 'tis highly entertaining to consider the judicious carelesness therein, really the grand gusto, like a great master in drawing, secure of the effect: a true master-piece. Every thing proper, bold, astonishing. The lights and shades adapted with inconceivable justness. Notwithstanding the monstrous size of the work, and every part of it; 'tis far from appearing heavy: 'tis compos'd of several species of work, and the proportions of the dissimilar parts recommend the whole, and it pleases like a magical spell. No one thinks any part of it too great or too little, too high or too low. And we that can only view it in its ruins, the less regret those ruins, that, if possible, add to its solemn majesty.

The stones of the gray weathers are of a bastard sort of white marble, and lie upon the surface of the ground, in infinite numbers, and of all dimensions. They are loose, detach'd from any rock, and doubtless lay there ever since the creation, being solid parts thrown out to the surface of the fluid globe, when its rotation was first impress'd. All our Druid temples are built, where these sort of stones from the surface can be had at reasonable distances; for they are never taken from quarries. Here is a very good quarry at *Chilmark* in this country. *Salisbury* cathedral, and all the great buildings are thence; but 'tis a stone quite different to our work. It was a matter of much labour to draw them hither, 16 miles. My friend the reverend Dr. *Stephen Hales*, the excellent author of vegetable statics, and other works, computed them as follows. The stone at the upper end of the cell, which is fallen down and broke in half, is in length (says he) 25 feet, in breadth 7 feet, and in thickness at a medium 3½, amounts to 612 cubic feet. Now a cubic foot of *Hedington* stone weighs near 154¼ pounds troy. If *Stonehenge* stone be of the same specific gravity, it will amount to 94,348 pounds, which is 31½ tuns. But is this be of the same specific gravity as *Burford* stone, which weighs to 155¼ the cubic foot, then it will weigh 95319 pounds troy, or 32 tuns. Is it be equal to *Blaidon* stone, which is 187 pounds troy *per* cubic foot, then it weighs 114,444 pounds troy, or 38 tuns. But I am sure that the stone is of considerably larger dimensions, than what Dr. *Hales* has stated it at, and that the sort of stone is much heavier than that of the largest specific gravity he speaks of, and that it amounts to more than 40 tuns, and requires more than 140 oxen to draw it; yet this is not the heaviest stone at the place.

The notion we ought to entertain of *Stonehenge* is not a little enhanc'd, by the discovery I made from frequent mensurations there. It gave me the opportunity of finding out the standard and original measure, which the people us'd, who made this and all other works of this kind. And this precludes any tedious disputation against the opinion of authors; for whoever makes any eminent building, most certainly forms it upon the common measure in use, among the people of that place. Therefore is the proportions of *Stonehenge* fall into fractions and uncouth numbers, when measur'd by the *English*, *French*, *Roman*, or *Grecian* foot, we may assuredly conclude, the architects were neither *English, French, Roman* or *Greeks*. Thus, for instance, when the accurate *Greaves* tells us, the door of the *Pantheon* (which is of one stone) is of *English* foot-measure 19 foot 603/1004 within: should we not be apt to assert at first sight, that the architect in so costly a work, did not chuse his measures at random, but intended that this dimension should be 20 feet? When we consider this building is at *Rome*, and that it amounts to 20 *Roman* feet, must we not conclude, it was erected by the *Roman* standard? adding too, that all the rest of the dimensions of this stately structure fall aptly and judiciously into the same scale. So as long as any *vestigia* of St. *Paul's* cathedral remain, the *English* foot, by which it was built, will easily be known. I must prepare the reader for a right understanding of our Druid edifices, by informing him, that *Stonehenge*, and all other works of this nature in our island, are erected by that most ancient measure call'd a cubit, which we read of in the holy scriptures, and in ancient profane authors. I mean the same individual measure, call'd the *Hebrew, Egyptian, Phœnician* cubit; most probably deriv'd from *Noah* and *Adam*. 'Tis the same that the pyramids of *Egypt* and other their works are projected upon; the same as that of *Moses's* tabernacle, *Solomon's* temple, *&c.* and we may reasonably pride ourselves in possessing these visible monuments of the old measure of the world. My predecessor Bishop *Cumberland* shows, enough to satisfy us, that the *Egyptian* and *Hebrew* measure was the same, tho' he has not hit upon that measure, to a nicety. My friend and collegue Dr. *Arbuthnot* has been more successful, in applying it to such parts of the greater pyramid, as evidently establish its proportion, to our English foot, from the measures *Greaves* has left us: and shows it to be 20 inches and 4/5 of *English* measure. Thus the Doctor observes the side of the greater pyramid at base, is 693 *English* feet; which amounts exactly to 400 *Egyptian* cubits, a full and suitable number for such a square work, and without question the originally design'd measure, the

*A View a little beyond Woodyates where the Ikening Street crosses part of a Druids barrow. Jun. 9, 1724.*

Plate 4. A View a little beyond Woodyates where the Ikening Street crosses part of a Druids barrow. Jun. 9, 1724.

*stadium* of old. I have taken notice that *Inigo Jones* observ'd the like dimensions, in laying out the plot of *Lincoln's-Inn-fields*. The Doctor adds many more instances, deduc'd in the same way, to confirm it. I add, that *Greaves* says, the lowermost steps of the pyramid are near 4 feet in height, which amounts to 2 cubits and 2 palms. They are 3 foot in breadth, *i.e.* 1 cubit 4 palms. The length of the declining first entrance is 92 feet and an half, *i.e.* 55 cubits. The length of the next gallery is 110 feet, which amounts to 60 cubits. There is another gallery in the pyramid, of the same length. Mr. *Webb* says the diameter of *Stonehenge* is 110 feet. This would tempt one to suspect the same measure us'd in both. Thus the diameter of the like work at *Rowldrich* in *Oxfordshire*, describ'd by Dr. *Plot*, is 35 yards, *i.e.* 110 feet, grossly measur'd. Father *Brothais* in his observations on upper *Egypt*, in our *Phil.*

26

*Trans.* found a door-case made of one stone, in a magnificent building, it was 26½ feet in height, this is 15 cubits. Dr. *Huntington*, in the same *Trans.* says, he found the sphinx standing by the northern pyramids to be 110 feet in circuit, *i.e.* 60 cubits. *Ptolomy* in his IVth book, and *Pliny* XXXVI. speak of the obelisk rais'd by king *Rameses* at *Heliopolis*, which Mr. *Webb*, p. 34. gives the length of in *English* feet, 136. This is 80 cubits. That which *Augustus* set up in the *circus maximus* at Rome upon reduction of *Egypt*, *Webb* says, is 120 feet 9 inches, which amounts to 70 cubits. Another, *Augustus* set up in the *campus martius*, which he says is 9 foot higher, *i.e.* 5 cubits. He speaks again of that erected by *Fontana* before St. *Peter*'s, 81 feet, which was 50 cubits. I suppose the base being injur'd, it was cut a little shorter. This at the base, he says, is 9 foot square, *i.e.* 5 cubits. The *Vatican* obelisk is 170 foot high, which is too cubits. 12 foot broad at bottom, which is 7 cubits; at top a third part less.

Hence we gather, the measure of the shew-bread table of the *Jews*, a cubit and half in height, *Exod.* xxv. 23. It had a golden crown about it, meaning a moulding, or verge or cornish, as upon our tea-tables. ר *peripheria, corona,* because 12 loaves were to be pil'd upon it. It was 31 inches in height, that of our ordinary eating-tables. And we shall find by this same cubit divided into its 6 tophach's or palms, all our Druid works are perform'd. 'Tis not to be wonder'd at, that it should come into *Britain*, with an eastern colony under the conduct of the *Egyptian, Tyrian, Phœnician Hercules*, (who was the same person) about *Abraham*'s time, or soon after, as I have good reasons to believe, which will be shown in its proper place.

# CHAP. II.

*Of the name of* Stonehenge. *These works prior to the* Roman *times. Who were the builders? Of the general situation of it, again. Of the beauty of its general proportion. A peep into it. A walk round the area.* Remarks on two stones standing on the vallum, *and two corresponding cavities for water vases: explained from ancient coins. That the* Welsh *are the remains of the* Belgæ *from the continent, who lived here at the* Roman *invasion, and by whose reports,* Stonehenge *was built by the most ancient oriental colony, that brought the* Druids *hither.*

COME we to the name of *Stonehenge,* so called by our *Saxon* ancestors; an argument sufficient, they were not the builders of it; they would have called it by a more honourable name. Rode hengenne is in *Saxon* a hanging-rod or pole, *i.e.* a gallows; and *Stonehenge* is a stone gallows, called so from the hanging parts, architraves, or rather imposts, the more remarkable part; and which only can persuade people from thinking, the stones *grew* in the very place, (as they express it.) And so Mr. *Camden,* Dr. *Holland,* Mr. *Webb* and others think, of the wonderful work at *Abury;* because there are none of these overthwart stones, as here. Many are so astonished at the bulk of these stones, that measuring all art and power by their own, they had rather think, they sprouted up in their places, like mushrooms, at regular distances, in mathematical circles; than that they were plac'd there by human industry, for excellent purpose. But pendulous rocks are now called *henges* in *Yorkshire,* and I have been informed of another place there called *Stonehenge,* being natural rocks. So that I doubt not, *Stonehenge* in *Saxon* signifies the hanging stones. In *Cornwall* is a Heath call'd now *Hengston* down, probably from such a work as ours, now demolished. It is in the hundred of *Easte.* And near it, is that other memorable Antiquity, composed of many upright stones, call'd the

Hurlers, a Druid temple. The old *Britons* or *Welsh* call *Stone-henge choir gaur*, which some interpret *chorea gigantum*, the giants dance: I judge, more rightly *chorus magnus*, the great choir, round church, or temple. As Banchor (where probably was of old, another Druid temple) means the high temple. But they mistake it for *chorea, chwarae χuare*, a ball, dance; as *Necham* sings;

> *Nobilis est lapidum structura, chorea gigantum:*
> *Ars experta, suum posse, peregit opus,*

Mr. *Camden* defines the work *coronæ in modum*. The Latin *co-rona* a crown, *corolla* a *ghirland*, and the *British crown* comes from its circular form, as *côr chorus*. The armoric *Britons* call *cryn rotundus, kruin* the *Irish*. *Coryn* is the round tip of any thing, many such like words in all the *Celtic* dialects. The *chorus* of a building among *Roman* christians, became appropriate to the more sacred part, or east end of churches, always turn'd of a circular form; from the time of *Constantine* the *Great*. Thus all the churches in the holy land, thus the chapel in *Colchester* castle, and in the *Tower* of *London,* (both, in my opinion, built about his time) are round at the east end. The old *Britons* or *Welsh*, we find, had a notion of its being a sacred place, tho' they were not the builders of it; for I take them to be the remains of the *Celtic* people that came from the continent, who chiefly inhabited *England*, at least the south part, when the *Romans* invaded the island, they are more particularly the remains of the *Belgæ*. I suppose their name *Welsh*, a corruption of *Belgæ*, Ὀυέλγαι in greek, 𝕭𝖊𝖑𝖌𝖎𝖘𝖈𝖍𝖊𝖓 and 𝕸𝖊𝖑𝖘𝖈𝖍𝖊𝖓 in german. *Strabo* IV. speaks of their way of making flannel, called λαιναȷ[λαῖνα, χλαῖνα for which our *Welsh* are so famous. *Strabo* gives the celtic word without the guttural aspirate, *chlæna* in latin. The most ancient inhabitants, the remains of the old *Phœnician* colony and primitive *Celts* who built *Stonehenge*, were the *Picts*, *Scots*, *Highland* and *Irish*, all the same people, tho' perhaps differing somewhat in dialect, as in situation: no otherwise than a *Cumberland-man* and one of *Somersetshire* now. The *Cornish*, I suppose, some remains too, of the old oriental race. But at this very day in *Wales*, they call every antiquated appearance beyond memory, *Irish*. Upon view of land, that from before any ones remembrance appears to have been plow'd, or very ancient ruins of buildings, and the like, they immediately pronounce, That it was in the times of the *Irish*. The very same is observable in the north, of the *Picts* or *Pights*, as they pronounce it, gutturally, in the oriental fashion, which we cannot imitate. They call old foundations, *Pights* houses, &c. Every thing is *Pictish*, whose origin they do not know. These people are conscious, that they are not the *Aborigines*, who by time and successive inundations, were forc'd northward and westward, into *Scotland* and *Ireland*. And also in the days of the *Romans*, such of the then inhabitants, as would not submit to their gentile yoke, took the same road.

The Front view of STONEHENGE.

Plate 5. The Front View of Stonehenge

The *Irish* therefore, or ancient *Scottish*, is the remnant of the *Phœnician* language, mixt with old *Biscayan* and *Gallic*, dialects of *Celts*; and some oriental, *Arabic* in particular: as Mr. *Toland* observes. And they are the descendants of the people who built *Stonehenge*, and the like Works. Whence spring the strange reports of these stones, coming from *Egypt*, from *Africa*, from *Spain*, from *Ireland*. As retaining some memory of the steps, by which the people who preceded their ancestors, travelled; nor they themselves, nor even the *Belgæ* pretending to be the builders of this wonderful work. For the *Belgæ* could not be ignorant of their own coming from the Gallic continent.

I have taken notice of another remarkable particular, as to the name of *Stonehenge*; which I apprehend to be of highest antiquity: that it was called the *Ambres*, or *Ambrose*, as the famous *main Ambre* by *Pensans* in *Cornwall*, another work of the Druids akin to this. And from hence the adjacent town of *Ambresbury* had its name. But of this matter, I must beg the readers patience, till I come to the last chapter, and discourse of the antiquity of there works in general.

So much at present as to the name of our fabrick; it is time to draw toward the sacred pile, and fancy ourselves walking upon this delightful plain:

--------------*juvat arva videre*
*Non rastris hominum, non ulli obnoxia curæ.* Virg.

nought can be sweeter than the air that moves o're this hard and dry, chalky soil. Every step you take upon the smooth carpet, (literally) your nose is saluted with the most fragrant smell of *serpillum*, and *apium*, which with the short grass continually cropt by the flocks of sheep, composes the softest and most verdant turf, extremely easy to walk on, and which rises as with a spring, under ones feet. The following drawing is a prospect taken from the king's barrow, west from

31

*Vespasian's* camp, in the way from *Ambresbury* to *Stonehenge*, by the *Bristol* road. Tho' the graver has not done it justice: yet it will give one a general notion of the situation of the place. It is admirably chosen, being in the midst of those wide downs, call'd *Salisbury* plain; between the river *Avon* to the east, and a brook that runs into the *Willy*, on the west. These two streams half round encompass it, at 2 miles distance, forming as it were a circular area, of 4 or 5 miles diameter, compos'd of gentle acclivities and declivities, open and airy. Yet agreeably diversify'd with the appearance of barrows, every where upon the edges of the highest grounds. Which very barrows are curious and entertaining, when view'd at hand, as well for the nicety and handsome turn of their forms, as for their great variety, and all within sight of the temple. These downs feed many flocks of sheep, and no doubt furnish'd the idea of *Thessalian* and *Arcadian* plains, to the noble *Sydney* residing at the neighbouring *Wilton*. The rivers are planted very thick with towns. Six miles south of *Stonehenge* is *Salisbury*, a mile nearer is *Sorbiodunum*, or old *Sarum*, by the side of which passes the *Roman* road via *Iceniana* reaching from *Norfolk*, into *Dorsetshire*. As this road goes southward, a mile beyond *Woodyates*, where it enters *Dorsetshire* and *Cranburn* chase, it passes over a heath where are many old barrows, like these on *Salisbury* plain. It happens there, to infringe upon one of the barrows, which luckily affords us a demonstration, of the road being made since those barrows; of which I took notice in my *itinerarium* p. 180. and further to gratify the curious have here inserted a print of it and may take the opportunity once for all to advertize them, of the disadvantage under which all drawings from these plains must appear. They are made for use and instruction, like mathematical figures, and cannot be expected much to please the eye; being form'd chiefly from bare lines, admitting no picture-like decoration.

I have observ'd another similar proof of these works being older than the *Roman* times here, in that *Roman* road that goes from *Marlborough* to *Bath*. It is near *Abury*, and I have a print of it engrav'd, which will be exhibited, when I next publish an account of that great work. But in the former, I call those Druid barrows, which are often found on these plains: a circular trench, sometime of 100 foot diameter, with only a small tump of earth in the middle, under which there is commonly an urn. Sometime two or three of these little tumps or diminutive *tumuli* within one circle, which it is natural to suppose, were friends or relations. These circles are always excellently well mark'd out.

The particular spot of ground where *Stonehenge* stands, is in the lordship of west or little *Ambresbury:* the possession of the reverend Mr. *Hayward*, who at present may be call'd the Archdruid of the island. 'Tis a delicate part of this large plain, with a gentle declivity from the south-west to the south and north-east. So that the soil, which is chalk, is perfectly dry and hard. Hence the infinite numbers of coaches and horses, that thro' so many centuries have been visiting the place every day, have not obliterated the track of the banks and ditches. The water cannot possibly rest any where hereabouts. The founders consulted well for the stability of their work, and salubrity of the place. *Cæsar* informs us in his commentaries, B. G. vi. 13. that among the Druids, "one has the supreme authority. When he is dead, whoever excels in dignity succeeds. But if there be more candidates, the Archdruid is chose by the votes of the Druids: and sometimes they fight for it. At a certain fix'd time of the year the *Gaulish* Druids meet, in the territories of the Carnutes, which country is in the middle of *Gaul, in a consecrated place.* Hither all persons from all quarters come, who have any controversy, and stand to their determination. The discipline of the Druids arose in *Britain*, and is said from thence to have been brought into *Gaul*. And now, they who design to be more throughly initiated therein, go over to learn." Here in few lines the great author acquaints us with a vast fund of ancient history, and upon which whole volumes have been wrote. I observe no more from it at present, than that we may very reasonably conclude, the elegant and the magnificent structure of *Stonehenge* was as the metropolitical church of the chief Druid of *Britain*. This was the *locus consecratus* where they met at some great festivals in the year, as well to perform the extraordinary sacrifices and religious rites, as to determine causes and civil matters. *Cæsar* calls these appointments of the Druids in *Gaul* consecrated places, where probably was nothing but a circle of rude stones. Had he seen those of our island, an *Abury* or even a *Stonehenge*, he would scarce have given them the title of temples: he was not used to the old patriarchal way. But I reckon the true reading in that passage quoted from him, to be *loco consecrato*, not *luco*, which was put in by some bold transcriber, who had heard of the fondness of the Druids for groves. But how unfit is a grove for a great and public meeting upon civil affairs? And this for the excellency of its situation upon a vast plain, was well calculated for a publick meeting of those of the order, at an election of a new Archdruid. As *Cæsar*'s words give light to the work before us, so it confirms what the warlike author says, of the discipline being originally in *Britain*; which the critics upon the continent cannot bear, and vainly endeavour to spirit away *Cæsar*'s meaning. The very building of *Stonehenge*, to say nothing of other like works here, shows it was not in vain, that the youth of *Gaul* came to learn of men, who could contrive and execute so mighty a work.

*Stonehenge* stands not upon the very summit of a hill, but pretty near it, and for more than three quarters of the circuit you ascend to it very gently from lower ground. At half a

34

mile distance, the appearance of it is stately and awful, really august. As you advance nearer, especially up the avenue, which is to the north-east of it, (which side is now most perfect) the greatness of its contour fills the eye in an astonishing manner is the front prospect from the entrance of the avenue. The stone that leans o'er the high attar appears thro' the grand or principal entrance: because we stand upon lower ground. If the reader pleases to cast his eye upon there 'tis represented in orthography, (to speak technically) as here in prospect. Hence by this method of comparing the designs together, we may, without confusion, gather a true notion of the work. *Stonehenge* is a good deal more in diameter, than the outside of St. *Paul*'s cupola.

| English Feet | Cubits | English Feet | Cubits | English Feet | Cubits | English Feet | Cubits | TAB.VI. |
|---|---|---|---|---|---|---|---|---|

Chart converting English feet to Cubits

And from a comparison of these two buildings, I was able to judge of the vanity of the architect of St. *Peter*'s at *Rome*, who in order to degrade the *Pantheon*, (whilst he was imitating it) boasted, he would set the *Pantheon* 200 foot high in the air, meaning the cupola there. But the architect of the *Pantheon*, *Valerius Ostiensis* (had he been alive) would have told him, that the vastness of the diameter in these cupola's is lost by the very height. Whatever we would have admired, ought to be preserved as the largest dimension. Therefore *Valerius*, with admirable judgment, has made the outward breadth of the *Pantheon* one fifth part compleatly longer than its height, taken in front; but if we measure it sidewise, taking in the portico, the breadth to the height, is more than 6 to 4. By this means the wonder of the *Pantheon*, the curve or arch 150 *Roman* feet in diameter, remains. So the curve of *Stonehenge*, which is above 100 *English* feet, appears extraordinary large and well proportion'd, upon a height of 18 foot, which reaches to the top of the outer cornish; that of the inner cornishes is but 24 foot high, at a medium. For the cornishes of the inner part of *Stonehenge*, or that which *Webb* calls the cell, are not all of equal height, of which in proper place. Thus both parts of the wonder is preserv'd, the greatness of the circuit of the whole work, the greatness and height of the parts that compose it; the height being one fourth of the diameter. The greatness too of the lights and shades in *Stonehenge*, as well as their variety arising from a circular form, gives it all possible advantage, and makes it deserve the appellation of;

*Deorum gloriosa domus,*

as *Theocritus* and *Herodotus* generally call temples. And its situation is correspondent to the antient notion. *Pausanias* praises the *Tanagrei* in *Beotia*, for having their temples in clean and distinct area's, distant from profane buildings and traffic.

*Stonehenge* is inclosed within a circular ditch. After one has pass'd this ditch, says the right reverend annotator to *Camden*, he ascends 35 yards before he comes at the work itself. This measure is the same, as that which Webb calls 110 foot, the diameter of the work. For the area inclos'd by a ditch, wherein *Stonehenge* is situate, is in diameter three times the diameter of *Stonehenge*. See the *Plate* of the *area*. Therefore the distance between the verge of the ditch within side, quite round, to the work of the Temple, is equal to the diameter of the Temple. The reader remembers what I promis'd, about the scale or measure whereby this work and all others of the Druids, is form'd; that 'tis the old *Hebrew*, *Phœnician* or *Egyptian* Cubit, which compar'd with the *English* foot, amounts to 20 inches and 4/5. Therefore I have drawn the ensuing comparison and proportion, between our *English* and *Hebrew* Scale; which is to accompany us in the future description the scale of cubits and feet compar'd. That I might not be suspected to savour an hypothesis, I produce other peoples measures, where I can find them in print, provided they be done with tolerable judgment and accuracy; for both are necessary in our case, with proper allowance. 'Tis not to be suppos'd, that in this work, the minuteness and extreme curiosity of *Desgodetz*, with which he measur'd the remains of old *Rome*, is expected, or even possible. For tho' the stones are not chizel'd and squar'd, to such preciseness, as *Roman* works are; yet they are chizel'd, and are far from rude. Nevertheless every body has not skill, properly to measure them. For they are much impair'd by weather: much is knock'd off by wretched hands. Those stones that stand, are luxated various ways, by time and their own weight; by silly people digging about them, and by the unfortunate colony of rabbets lately translated thither. So that we may well say with *Claudian*,

> *Seram ponderibus pronis tractura ruinam,*
> *Pars cadit affiduo flatu, pars imbre peresa*
> *Rumpitur, abripuit partem vitiosa vetustas.*

I was forc'd to make many admeasurements and repeated, before I could obtain an exact ground-plot; and it requir'd much consideration to do it, and to find out the true scale by which it was compos'd, the Druid cubit, which they TAB. VI. brought with them from the east. Therefore by the annexed scales which I have contriv'd to answer all lengths, the reader. will most perfectly understand the subsequent description, and see the truth of my assertion: and may from thence be enabled to measure any other like works, in our islands, which I have not had the opportunity of viewing. It was the eastern way, in laying out a building, to use a staff of 6 cubits long. This was of a convenient, manageable length; and its divisions being half a dozen, suited well a reckoning by duodenaries. Thus in *Ezek.* xl. 3, S. *Apoc.* xxi. 16. the angel that laid out the temple of *Solomon*, is described, as having a reed of 6 cubits (a measuring reed or cane) in his hand. This being the universal and first measure of antiquity, was in time spread all over the world. In particular, it became the *decempedum* of the *Greeks* and *Romans*; the common measuring standard. But 'tis remarkable, they alter'd the divisions, thinking it more artful and convenient to have them in less parts: and instead of 6 cubits, they made it consist of 10 feet. And by time and change, the whole measure became somewhat alter'd from the primitive. For the *Greek decempedum* was swell'd somewhat too long, as the *Romans* diminish'd theirs a little. Ezekiel's reed is our 10 foot and 4 inches 2/3; 400 cubits is the *stadium* of the ancients, or furlong, 100 feet.

When you enter the building, whether on foot or horseback and cast your eyes around, upon the yawning ruins, you are struck into an exstatic *reverie*, which none can describe, and they only can be sensible of, that feel it. Other buildings fall by piece meal, but here a single stone is a ruin, and lies like the haughty carcase of *Goliath*. Yet there is as much of it undemolished, as enables us sufficiently to recover its form, when it was in its most perfect state. There is enough of every part to preserve the idea of the whole. The next peep (as I call it) into the *sanctum sanctorum*, is drawn, at the very entrance, and as a view into the inside. When we advance further, the dark part of the ponderous imposts over our heads, the chasm of sky between the jambs of the cell, the odd construction of the whole, and the greatness of every part, surprizes. We may well cry out in the poet's words

*Tantum Relligio potuit!*

if you look upon the perfect part, you fancy intire quarries mounted up into the air: if upon the rude havock below, you see as it were the bowels of a mountain turn'd inside outwards. It is pleasant likewise to consider the spot upon which 'tis situate, and to take a circular view of the country around it. For which purpose I have sketch'd the following prospects, taking in the country almost round the circumference of the horizon. This Use there will be in them further; is ever it happen, that this noble work should be destroy'd: the spot of it may be found, by these views.

Plate 7. A peep into the Sanctum Sanctorum

The *vallum* of the ditch which incloses the *area*, or court, is inwards, and makes a circular terras; walking upon which, we take the foregoing prospects. The lowest part of the *area* is towards the entrance. The tops of all the circumjacent hills, or rather easy elevations, are cover'd o're, as it were, with barrows, which cause an agreeable appearance; adorning the bare downs with their figures. And this ring of barrows reaches no further, than till you lose sight of the temple, or thereabouts. Stand at the grand entrance by the stone that lies upon the ground, and the view of the temple presents itself as in the the front prospect of *Stonehenge*. Directly down the avenue, to the north-east, the apex of an hill terminates the horizon, between which and the bottom of a valley you see the *Cursus*, a work which has never yet been taken notice of. Being a space of ground included between two long banks going parallel east and west, at 350 foot distance, the length 10000 feet. This was design'd for the horse races and games, like the *Olympic*, the *Isthmian*, &c. of the *Greeks*. But we shall speak more particularly of this afterwards. In the valley on this side of it, the strait part of the avenue terminates in two branches; that on the left hand, leads to the *Cursus*; that on the right goes directly up the hill, between two famous groups of barrows, each consisting of seven in number. The farthest, or those northward, I call the oldest king's barrows; the hithermost are vulgarly called the seven king's graves.

If we walk a little to the left hand is presented. See the northern long barrow: on this side of which, the eye takes in the whole length of the *Cursus*. Many barrows at the end and on both sides of it. That mark'd P. was open'd by my Lord *Pembroke*, those mark'd S. were open'd by myself. What was discover'd therein will be treated of hereafter. Further to the west, the highest ground of that spot whereon *Stonehenge* stands, eclipses a distant view, and *there* are the nearest barrows planted with rabbets, which do much damage too at *Stonehenge*, and threaten no less than the ruin of the whole. Upon the *vallum* of *Stonehenge* is one of the stones there, which seems to be a small altar, for some kind of libations, and at the letter A. the mark of a cavity; of which more particularly, in the next page. The next or south-west prospect from *Stonehenge*, takes in the country from *Berwickbarn*, and my Lord *Pembroke*'s wood of *Groveley*, to *Salisbury* steeple: a chain of barrows reaching a 6th part of the whole horizon.

Many from the great quantity of these sepulchral *tumuli* here, injudiciously conclude, that there have been great battels upon the plain, and that the slain were bury'd there. But they are really no other than family burying-places, set near this temple, for the same reason as we bury in church-yards yards and consecrated ground. *Salisbury* steeple seen from hence, brings to my sorrowful remembrance, the great *Thomas* Earl of *Pembroke*, whose noble ashes are there deposited. He was patron of my studies, particularly those relating to *Stonehenge*. Virtue, piety, magnanimity, learning, generosity, all sublime qualities recommended and added to his illustrious descent. Glorious it will be for me, if these pages live to testify to another age, the intimacy he was pleased to honour me with.

------------*quis talia fando*
*Temperet a lachrymis---------- --------!*

In this *Plate*, the reader may remark another of the cavities within the *vallum*, to which that corresponds on the opposite diameter before hinted at.

The south-east prospect finishes the circle looking towards the valley southward, where the rain-water passes, from the whole work of *Stonehenge*, the whole tract of the *Cursus* and the country beyond it, as far as north long barrow; and so is convey'd into the river *Avon* at *Lake*. That road between king barrow and the seven barrows is the way to *Vespasian*'s camp and so to *Ambresbury*. The barrow under those seven kings of later form, is that nearest to *Stonehenge*.

Doubtless in the sacrifices and ceremonies which were here practis'd, water was us'd, and I observe most of our Druid temples are set near rivers. The reason why *Stonehenge* was not set near a river, has hitherto effectually preserv'd it, this

43

part being uninhabitable upon that account, and rather too far off a town for tillage. But when I curiously contemplated the beauty and convenience of this court, I observ'd two remarkable places, which plainly have a conformity with the two stones set upon the *vallum*; which stones puzzle all enquirers. Those particulars seem to explain one another, and more especially by the help of a coin in *Vaillant*, tom. II. p. 240. for which reason I caus'd it to be engraven on that plate the *area* of *Stonehenge*. 'Tis a coin of *Philip* the *Roman* emperor, struck by the city of *Heliopolis* in *Cœlesyria* under mount *Libanus*, now call'd *Baldec*, where is an admirable ancient temple remaining, describ'd and pictur'd in *Maundrel*'s travels of the holy land. In the walls of it are two or three stones of an immense length, which seem to be the fragments of an obelisk, dedicated to the sun, whence the name of *Heliopolis*. The coin presents a temple built upon a rock: to which they ascend by steps. The temple is inclos'd in an *area* with a wall. On the left hand by the circuit of the *area* is a stone altar. A little further, is a great vase for water to be us'd in the sacrifices. The legend is COL*onia* IVL*ia* AVG*usta* FEL*ix* HEL*iopolitana*. Now the two cavities in the circuit of our *area*, very probably were the places where two great stone vases were set, and the two stones were two altars for some particular rites, which we don't take upon ourselves to explain. See another coin II. in *Descamp's selectiora numismata*, p. 23. which is to the same purpose. Those stones are set in their proper places in my scheme of the *area* of *Stonehenge:* and I leave them to the better conjectures of the learned in these matters. Mr. *Webb* fancies them the jambs of two portals of two entrances, besides the great entrance; and makes them favour his imaginary triangles, from which he forms the work of *Stonehenge*, upon a *Vitruvian* plan. And in order to bring this about, he draws one stone, that toward the east, or on the left hand, from the true and only entrance, no less than 120 foot out of its real place. No doubt, the reader will be surpriz'd at this, and the easier credit me, when I say his ground-plot in other parts, is very far from being exact. The reader will observe from my scheme, that the two semicircular hollows mark'd A A, wherein I suppose the water-vases were set, are plac'd alternatively, with the two stones: I don't pretend to show why the Druids did so. But that stone standing, together with the upper A, and the center of the grand entrance by the stone that lies flat there, make an exact equilateral triangle; yet really have not the lean relation to the scheme of the work of *Stonehenge* in general, or to the cell in particular. Nor do the stones, or those hollows, point out any other entrance cross the ditch into the *area*. So in the tabernacle of *Moses* and temple of *Solomon*, great vases in brass were set for water, in the court before the temple.

Plate 8. North Prospect from Stonehenge
P. a barrow opened by Lord Pembroke. S. by W. Stukeley.

# CHAP. III.

*The admeasurement of the ground-plot; and outer circle of the temple, and imposts over it. Of the principal line of the work, running down the avenue, and single entrance, into the area, or court. The imposts are jointed exquisitely by mortaise and tenon. The temple at Persepolis a building of this sort.*

LET us now set about an examination of the measures of the temple itself. Take a staff 10 foot 4 inches and ¾ long. Divide it into six equal parts. These are the cubits of the ancients. Each cubit is divided into six parts. These are palms. Thus have we the original measure of the founders of *Stonehenge*. We will take Mr. *Webb's* measures, and compare 'em herewith the ground-plot.

Mr. *Webb* says, p. 55. that the whole work of *Stonehenge* being of a circular form, is 110 foot in diameter. But to be precise, 'tis 108 and somewhat more, and his own scale in his ground-plot shows the same. This is the diameter from outside to outside, which in our ground-plot is the principal diameter. The thickness of the stones of the outward circle, he says, p. 59. are 3 foot and an half. Hence the inner diameter becomes almost 102 feet English. If the reader pleases to measure 102 feet upon the comparative scales, which I gave of the *English* foot and *Hebrew* cubit, being the measure us'd by the Druids, or in the scales at the bottom of the ground-plot, he will find that it amounts exactly to 60 cubits. 30 cubits being the *radius* wherewith they struck the circle upon the turf, which is the inner circumference of that work. *That* sufficiently defin'd their ground-plot. For tho' they intended in general, that the thickness of the stones of this outer circle should be 3 foot and a half; but to speak more properly, 2 cubits (which is the same measure) yet they were more careful of one side only, of that dimension. And the chief business being withinside this temple, they set the best face of the stones inwards, upon that ground-line; the other face was suited as well as the scantlings they could get, best answer'd. *Webb's* 3 foot and a half is precisely 3 foot 5 inches, and somewhat more, making compleatly 2 Druid cubits, as you find by the scales. They that carefully view *Stonehenge*, will easily see, that the stones of the inside both of the outward circle and of the cell, are the smoothest, best wrought, and have the handsomest appearance. For so the polite architects of the eastern part of the world, bestow'd more elegance within their temples than without. Not as our modern *London* builders, who carve every moulding, and crowd every ornament, which they borrow out of books, on the outside of our publick structures, that they may more commodiously gather the dust and smoke. The truth is, good sense and observation of nature, produces the same ideas in all ages and all nations. Our Druids observ'd, that God almighty in forming the body of a man, made all the external parts great, bold, round, with ornament sufficient; but where the beauty chiefly consisted in the fitness of the proportions, in symmetry and plainness. In the inside, he has display'd all the *minutiæ* of divine skill. They have done the like, according to their way, in *Stonehenge*. So even as to the outward appearance, I find they took care to set those stones that had the best outward face, toward the front or entrance. And to embarrass the general scheme of the work, they made use of two centers instead of one, but 2 cubits distance from one another; perhaps to make the thing intricate and as magical: besides the advantage it gives to the oval form of the included cell.

Observe, in laying down the ground-plot and projecting this outer circle, we said it was 110 feet, (gross measure) in diameter. We remember what is before-mention'd, that the learned *Greaves* measur'd two galleries in the greater pyramid, in like manner, each 110 feet. So the bishop of London says, from the grand entrance of *Stonehenge*, to the work is 35 yards: so he says the diameter of the circle at *Rowldrich* in *Oxfordshire*, is 35 yards: all this while 60 Druid or Egyptian cubits are meant. So the length of *Solomon*'s temple was 60 cubits, whereof the *Ædes* 40 cubits, the *sanctum sanctorum* 20.

The intention of the founders of *Stonehenge* was this. The whole circle was to consist of 30 stones, each stone was to be 4 cubits broad, each interval 2 cubits. 30 times 4 cubits is twice 60: 30 times 2 cubits is 60. So that thrice 60 cubits compleats a circle whose diameter is 60. A stone being 4 cubits broad, and 2 cubits thick is double the interval, which is a square of 2 cubits. Change the places between the stones and their intervals, and it will make a good ground-plot for a circular portico of *Greek* or *Roman* work. For supposing these intervals to be square plinths of 2 cubits each side, and columns properly set upon them: it will admit of 3 diameters for the intercolumniation, which is the diastyle manner in architecture. But to talk of pycnostyle with Mr. *Webb*, and call these stones of ours pillars or pillasters, where they are twice as broad as the space between them, and to call this an order, is monstrous.

Thus a stone and an interval in this outward circle of *Stonehenge*, makes 3 squares; 2 allotted to the stone, 1 to the interval; which for stability and beauty withal, in such a work as ours, is a good proportion. The curiosity of the work, and the general orthography of the outward circle, I have design'd in and it may be seen in the seven stones now remaining at the grand entrance. Which show what strictly was the intent of the founders, and where they took the liberty to relax of that strictness, and that with judgment; so as to produce a good effect. I shall explain it from Mr. *Webb's* own measures, that I may give the truth its full advantage. P. 59. he says, the stones which made the outward circle are 7 foot in breadth. Observe that 7 foot makes 4. cubits of the Druids. He says, they are 15 foot and a half high. You find that exactly 9 cubits. P. 61. he says, the architraves lying round about upon them, are 2 foot and a half high, *i.e.* our cubit and half. He mentions their breadth to be 3 foot and half; equal to the thickness of the upright, *i.e.* our two cubits. They are jointed in the middle of each perpendicular stone. Hence tho' he has not mention'd the length of these architraves, we gather them to be 6 cubits long. This is spoke of their inward length, for outwardly they must needs be somewhat longer, as being an ark of a larger circle. I must observe about these architraves, as Mr. *Webb* calls them, that they are more properly call'd imposts or cornishes; for they are not made to support any thing above them, as is the nature of an architrave, but for the stability and ornament of what supports them, which is the nature of imposts and cornishes. Tho' these bodies of stone here, never had or were intended to have, any mouldings upon them, like *Greek* and *Roman* works; they are wrought perfectly plain, and suitable to the stones that support them. I observe further, the chizeling of our upright stones, is only above ground. For the 4 or 5 foot in length below ground, is left in the original natural form. And that the upright stones are made very judiciously to diminish a little, every way; so that at top they are but 3 cubits and a half broad, and so much narrower as to suffer their imposts, to hang over a little, or project (in properer terms) over the heads of the uprights, both within side and without. By this means these uprights are in much less danger of falling or swerving any way: and the imposts, which are not broader than the thickness of the stones at bottom, which support them, have a graceful effect, by projecting a little, without danger of surcharging them. We see here plain, natural, easy geometry, what we may call the

Plate 9. Southwest Prospect from Stonehenge
A. The barrow L$^d$. Pembroke open'd. BB. those I open'd. C. Bushbarrow. D. a cavity in the vallum.

first rudiment of art, deduc'd from common reason: but they that can find any *Roman* delicacy herein, must, I freely own, have a much nicer eye and talk, than I can pretend to. The Druids had, from patriarchal times, made their altars or temples of rude unpolish'd stones. But now hearing, probably from *Phœnician* traders, of the glories of *Solomon*'s temple, at least of other temples made artfully in imitation of it; such as those of *Sesostris* in *Egypt*, and others about *Phœnicia*: they thus made a small approach to square scantlings and stones wrought. And this seems to have been the first and the last work of theirs of this kind, that I can hear of, either in the *Britanic* isles, or on the continent. And no doubt but it must give them so high a reputation, that even the people of *Gaul* themselves could not help owning to *Cæsar*, that the discipline of these men was first begun here, and carry'd on with such success, that they sent their youth from the continent hither, as to an academy, to be initiated in their learning. We are not to suppose these words are to be strictly taken, as if the Druids here began their institution: but that being an oriental manner of religion, and much different from that on the *Gallic* continent, what they had of it there, was deriv'd from *Britain*. It appear'd as much new to them, who were chiefly idolaters, as in many ages preceding, *Abraham*'s religion appear'd new to the inhabitants of *Phœnicia* and *Egypt:* who were then not much tinctur'd with idolatry. Nor, probably, had the Druids much opportunity of building another such work, as *Stonehenge*, between its foundation and the *Roman* times. Because, I apprehend, the encroachments of the *Gallic* nations from the continent, seating themselves in *Britain*, about 200 years before *Cæsar*'s invasion, had molested the Druids much, in these southern counties: and drove them with the old *Britons*, farther northward and westward. But of this we will treat more particularly afterwards, when we offer our opinion, of the time when it was made.

In the orthographic plate we may see the strict geometry of the work of this outward circle, and the artful variation therefrom, in order to make the aperture of the grand entrance somewhat wider than the rest. Mr. *Webb* does not take notice of this particular; and he might have triumph'd in it. For 'tis no less than a *Vitruvian* rule, to relax the intercolumniation just in the middle of the portico, in the front of a temple, and over-against the door. He speaks of it in *Lib.* III. 2. when talking of the *Eustyle ratio*, the best for use, appearance and strength: he directs the intercolumniation to be of two diameters and ¼; but the middle intercolumniation of three diameters. By which means the approach to the door will be much more commodious, and nothing diminish'd of beauty in aspect. And this is the reality of the case before us.

But alas, our *British* priests knew nothing of *Vitruvius;* they deduc'd this knack from an authority much ancienter than him, *viz.* from pure natural reason, and good sense. Nor does this hurt the whole of the work. The aperture ought strictly to have been two cubits equal to the rest, but they advanc'd it to two cubits and a half. This only crowds the next intervals on each side a small matter nearer, the rest preserving their true distance quite round. And in the work itself, 'tis obvious enough to the naked eye. Again, there is another remarkable particular observ'd by our priests. Because the aperture of the principal entrance we are speaking of, is wider than the rest: they have made the impost over it thicker than the rest, and 'tis equally obvious to the naked eye. This was the more effectually to secure it from breaking. But this additional thickness they have put below. They were sensible it would have produc'd an ill effect at top, by breaking the line of that noble cincture. It must be own'd this was extremely well adjusted. And the breadth of the stone that hangs over head in this place is astonishing. I had the greatest pleasure imaginable, in the year 1723, *July*, in being here for several days together, with the learned *Heneage* Lord *Winchelsea*. I have just reason to boast of that intimacy he indulg'd me in; and his memory must for ever be dear to me, for his noble qualities. My Lord and I were very careful in taking the measures of *Stonehenge*; and with great grief we observ'd, the stones here represented in that Plate and the front view, to be much deviated forwards from their true perpendicular, and in the utmost danger of falling. 'Tis to be fear'd some indiscreet people have been digging about the great entrance, with ridiculous hopes of finding treasure, and loosen'd thereby the chalky foundation. We found by measure, that the upper edge of the impost overhangs no less than 2 foot 7 inches, which is very considerable in a height of 18. The whole breadth at the foundation is but 3 foot and a half. And this noble front is now chiefly kept up by the masonry of the mortaise and tenon of the imposts.

Thro' the middle of the principal entrance, runs the principal line of the whole work; the diameter from north-east to south-west. This line cuts the middle of the altar, length of the cell, the entrance, the entrance into the court, and so runs down the middle of the avenue, to the bottom of the valley for almost 2000 feet together. This is very apparent to any one at first sight, and determines this for the only principal entrance of the temple. All the other intervals of the stones of the outer circle, have no preheminence in any respect. There is no such thing as three entrances, which Mr. *Webb's* scheme suggests. He might as well have pretended there are 6, for so many points of his triangles meet in intervals, at the verge of the outer circle. Upon this line are all the principal centers that compose the work, it varies a small matter from true north-east.

The contrivance of our artificers in making mortaises and tenons, between the upright stones and the imposts is admirable, but so contrary to any practice of the *Romans*, that it alone is enough to disqualify their claim to the work. Much judgment and good sense is shewn in the management of them. The centers of the tenons are 2 cubits distant from each other, upon each upright. By this means there is 4 cubits distance from the center of the tenon of one stone, to the center of the tenon of its next neighbour, across the intervals, or in one impost. Divide the upper face of an upright into its 2 squares, the center of a tenon is in the center of that square. Divide the under face of an impost, into its 3 squares, the correspondent mortaises are in the centers of the two outermost squares, and this was the strict geometrical method us'd by the founders: so that the stones fitted, as soon as plac'd in their true situations. These tenons and mortaises of this outer circle are round, and fit one another very aptly. The tenons and mortaises, are to inches and a half in diameter, which is 3 palms, or half a cubit. They rather resemble half an egg, than an hemisphere. These most effectually keep both uprights and imposts from luxation, and they must have used great labour that threw them down. Sir *Robert Sibbald* speaks of a rocking stone in *Ireland*, contriv'd with mortaise and tenon like ours: of which Mr. *Toland* gives us an account, with other like, the works of the Druids.

The whole height of upright and impost is 10 cubits and a half. The uprights 9 cubits, the impost 1 cubit and a half, so that the impost is a 6th part of the height of the upright. If we measure on the outside, the collective breadth of two upright stones, and the interval between them, 'tis 10 cubits and a half equal to the whole height; and the interval is half the breadth of a stone, the thickness of a stone is half its breadth. That impost which lies over the grand entrance, we said, was deeper and longer than the rest. *Abraham Sturges* an architect, and myself measured it, in presence of Lord *Winchelsea*. Its middle length is 11 feet 10 inches, which is 6 cubits 4 palms; 2 foot 11 inches high, which is 1 cubit 4 palms. They have likewise added a little to its breadth, more than the rest, being 3 foot 9 inches, which is 2 cubits and a palm. *N. B.* The scale of my drawing is adapted for the inside of the circle, upon which the proportions in geometry are built: so that the outward breadths of the uprights and

Plate 10. South-East Prospect from Stonehenge

54

lengths of the imposts are somewhat more, than by the scale appears there. The intelligent reader knows this must be the consequence, in arks of a larger circle.

Nothing in nature could be of a more simple idea than this vast circle of stones, and its crown-work or *corona* at top; and yet its effect is truly majestic and venerable, which is the main requisite in sacred structures. A single stone is a thing worthy of admiration, but the boldness and great relievo of the whole *compages*, can only be rightly apprehended, from view of the original. On the outside, the imposts are rounded a little to humour the curvity of the circle, and within they are strait, tho' they ought to be a little curv'd. This makes them somewhat broader in the middle, than at the end, and broader than the 2 cubits, which is the thickness of the upright stones, upon an ichnography. So that within, the crown-work makes a polygon of 30 sides. But this little artifice without debating the beauty of the work in the least, adds much strength to the whole, and to the imposts in par-ticular. We may guess their proportions are well chose, when so many of them are thrown down by violence, and not broke in the fall. And their greater breadth in the middle, or that part that covers the intervals, adds to the solemnity of the place, by the shadow they present at the bottom. The whole affair of jointing in this building is very curious, and seems to be the oldest and only specimen of this kind of work in the world. There is nothing, that I know of, comes in competition with it, but the celebrated ruins at *Persepolis*. It is compos'd of great stones laid across one another, as *Stone-henge*: but not with mortaise and tenon. The vulgar and learned too, generally take it for the remains of the palace of the *Persian* monarchs, burnt by *Alexander* the great; but it is really an open temple like ours, and made much in the same manner. But the stones are well squar'd, ornamented with mouldings and carvings, and the whole of them are squares, not round works as here. *Persepolis* is a mixture, between the ancient patriarchal round form of open temples, and the square form introduc'd under the *Jewish* dispensation, in opposition to the former, which were generally degenerated into idolatrous purposes. But of this I shall speak more perhaps hereafter, when I treat of the most ancient temples.

Of the outer circle at *Stonehenge* which in its perfection consisted of 60 stones, 30 uprights and 30 imposts, there are more than half the uprights, *viz.* 17 left standing. 11 of these uprights remain, continuous, by the grand entrance, five imposts upon them. One upright at the back of the temple or on the south-west, leans upon a stone of the inner circle. There are six more lying upon the ground, whole or in pieces. So that 24 out of 30 are still visible at the place. There is but one impost more in its proper place. And but two lying upon the ground, so that 22 are carried off. Hence I infer, this temple was not defac'd when christianity prevailed. But some rude and sacrilegious hands carried the stones away for other uses. However it cannot but be the highest pleasure imaginable to a regular mind, to walk round and contemplate the stately ruins which I have endeavour'd to preserve in the outside views, such as from the south-west, and so of the rest. But we may say with *Lucan*,

*Jam magis atque magis præceps agit omnia fatum.*

# CHAP. IV.

*Of the lesser circle of stones, without imposts. A disputation again Mr. Webb.*

MANY drawings have been made and publish'd, of *Stonehenge*. But they are not done in a scientific way, so as may prove any point, or improve our understanding in the work. I have therefore drawn four architectonic orthographies: one is of the front and outside: three are different sections upon the two principal diameters of the work. These will for ever preserve the memory of the thing, when the ruins even of these ruins are perish'd; because from them and the ground-plot, at any time, an exact model may be made these orthographies show the primary intent of the founders; they are the designs, which the Druids made, before they put the work in execution. And by comparing them with the drawings correspondent, of the ruins, we gain a just idea of the place, when it was in its perfection. But now as we are going to enter into the building, it will be proper again to survey the ground-plot, which is so different from that publish'd by Mr. *Webb*. Instead of an imaginary hexagon, we see a most noble and beautiful ellipsis, which composes the cell, as he names it, I think *adytum* a proper word. There is nothing like it, to my knowledge, in all antiquity; and 'tis an original invention of our Druids, an ingenious contrivance to relax the inner and more sacred part, where they perform'd their religious offices. The two outward circles do not hinder the sight, but add much to the solemnity of the place and the duties, by the crebrity and variety of their intervals. They that were within, when it was in perfection, would see a most notable effect produc'd by this elliptical figure, included in a circular *corona*, having a large hemisphere of the heavens for its covering.

Somewhat more than 8 feet inward, from the inside of this exterior circle, is another circle of much lesser stones. In the measure of the Druids 'tis five cubits. This circle was made by a radius of 24 cubits, drawn from the common centers of the work. This struck in the chalk the line of the circumference wherein they set these stones. The stones that compote it are 40 in number, forming with the outward circle (as it were) a circular portico: a most beautiful walk, and of a pretty effect. Somewhat of the beauty of it may be seen where, at present, 'tis most perfect. We are impos'd on, in Mr. *Webb's* scheme, where he places only 30 stones equal to the number of the outer circle, the better to humour his fancy of the dipteric aspect, p. 76. He is for persuading us, this is a *Roman* work compos'd from a mixture of the plainness and solidity of the Tuscan order, with the delicacy of the Corinthian. That in aspect 'tis *dipteros hypæthros*, that in manner 'tis *pycnostylos*; which when apply'd to our antiquity, is no better than playing with words. For suppose this inner circle consisted of only 30 stones, and they set as in his scheme, upon the same *radius*, as those of the outer: what conformity has this to a portico properly, to an order, *tuscan, corinthian* or any other, what similitude is there between these stones and a column? where one sort is square oblong, the other opposite (by his own account) pyramidal. Of what order is a column, or rather a pilaster, where its height is little more than twice its diameter? Where is the base, the shaft, the capital, or any thing that belongs to a pillar, pillaster or portico? the truth and fact is this. The inner circle has 40 stones in it. Whence few or none but those two intervals upon the principal diameter, happen precisely to correspond with those of the outer circle. Whereby a much better effect is produc'd, than if the case had been as *Webb* would have it. For a regularity there, would have been trifling and impertinent. Again, Mr. *Webb* makes these stones pyramidal in shape, without reason. They are truly flat parallelograms, as those of the outer circle. He says, p. 59. they are one foot and a half in breadth, but they are twice as much.

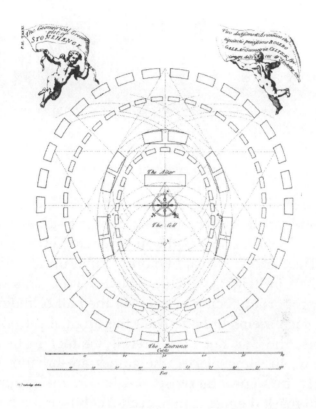

Plate 11. The Geometrical Ground plot of Stonehenge

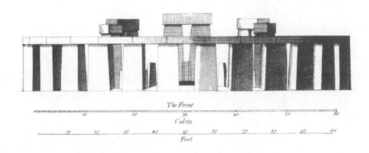

Plate 12. The Orthography of Stonehenge

Their general and designed proportion is 2 cubits, or two cubits and a half, as they happen'd to find suitable stones. A radius of 23 cubits strikes the inner circumference: of 24 the outer. They are, as we said before, a cubit thick, and 4 cubits and a half in height, which is above 7 foot. This was their stated proportion, being every way the half of the outer uprights. Such seems to have been the original purpose of the founders, tho' 'tis not very precise, neither in design, nor execution. In some places, the stones are broader than the intervals, in some otherwise: so that in the ground-plot I chose to mark them as equal, each 2 cubits and a half. There are scarce any of these intire, as to all these dimensions; but from all, and from the symmetry of these *Celtic* kind of works, which I have been conversant in, I found this to be the intention of the authors. 'Tis easy for any one to satisfy themselves, they never were pyramidal; for behind the upper end of the *adytum*, there are three or four left, much broader than thick, above twice; and not the least semblance of a pyramid. I doubt not but he means an obelisk, to which they might some of them possibly be likened, but not at all

to a pyramid. Nor indeed do I imagine any thing of an obelisk was in the founders view; but the stones diminish a little
upward, as common reason dictates they ought to do. Nor
need we bestow the pompous words of either pyramid, or
obelisk upon them. For they cannot be said to imitate, either
one or other, in shape, use, much less magnitude: the chief
thing to be regarded, in a comparison of this sort. The central
distance between these stones of the inner circle, measured
upon their outward circumference, is 4 cubits. I observe further, that the two stones of the principal entrance of this circle, correspondent to that of the outer circle, are broader and
taller, and set at a greater distance from each other, being
rather more than that of the principal entrance in the outer
circle. It is evident too, that they are set somewhat more inward than the rest; so as that their outward face stands on
the line that marks the inner circumference of the inner circle. I know no reason for all this, unless it be, that the outside
of these two stones, is the outside of the hither end of the ellipsis of the *adytum:* for so it corresponds by measure upon
the ground-plot. This is apparent, that they eminently point
out the principal entrance of that circle, which is also the entrance into the *adytum.* For five stones on this hand, and five
on that, are as it were the *cancelli* between the *sanctum* and
*sanctum sanctorum,* if we may use such expressions. 'Tis
scarce worth mentioning to the reader, that there never were
any imposts over the heads of these stones of the inner circle.
They are sufficiently fasten'd into the ground. Such would
have been no security to them, no ornament. They are of a
harder kind of stone than the rest, as they are lesser; the better to resist violence.

There are but nineteen of the whole number left; but eleven
of them are standing *in situ.* There are five in one place
standing contiguous, three in another, two in another. The
walk between these two circles, which is 300 foot in circum-

ference, is very noble and very delightful. Probably it gave *Inigo Jones* the idea of designing that fine circular portico, which is one great beauty, among many, in his drawings for *White-hall*, publish'd lately from the originals by my Lord *Burlington*; who has a true notion of the extraordinary merit of that great man: and very commendably has reviv'd his memory. Such a circular portico put in execution, would have a marvellous effect, much exceed a common gallery in use, because 'tis a perpetual walk, without turning back, and well becomes a royal residence. The best view of this sort, to be had from our work, is from the north, as in the reader cannot TAB. XVII. but observe, how little pretence here is for an imitation of *Greek* or *Roman* portico's, notwithstanding the grand and agreeable curve of the outward circle. But when we see the disproportion of the inner circle in regard to any purpose of this sort, we must own the invention of *Hermogenes* in contriving the *pseudo-dipteros*, is here apply'd with an ill grace. The founders of *Stonehenge* cou'd have no need of make-shifts for want of room on Salisbury plain. Or how could a concentric row of little stones, or pillars if he will so have it, bear any resemblance to the contrivance of *Hermogenes*, which consisted in having none; in taking away the whole inner row of pillars, so as to add to the convenience of room, and preserve the aspect, at the same time? Most undoubtedly the Druids had no further meaning in it, than to make use of the even numbers of 30 greater stones, and 40 lesser stones; and this was to produce a more perplexed variety, by the interstices having no regard to one another. So far were they from having a notion of *Grecian* beauty, in the pillars of circular portico's being set on the same *radius*; pillar answering to pillar, intercolumniation to intercolumniation. And this will be shown repeatedly in the progress of this work, to be the common practice of the Druids in other like instances.

But when we consider the cell, as Mr. *Webb* names it, we find him guilty of great disingenuity, in ill conceiving the form of it, and in distorting his ground-plots, to colour it over the better. The minute you enter this *adytum* as in you discover 'tis not a hexagon, nor ever was intended for one, and there can be no greater absurdity than to imagine it one. It is in truth compos'd of certain *compages* of stones, which I shall call *trilithons*, because made, each of two upright stones, with an impost at top: and there are manifestly 5 of these *trilithons* remaining. But the naked eye easily discovers, they are very far from making 5 sides of a hexagon. They cannot be brought to any approach, of a truly circular polygon. 3 *trilithons* of the 5 are remaining entire, 2 are ruin'd indeed, in some measure, but the stones remain *in situ*. And nothing is easier, than to take the ground-plot, from symmetry and correspondency. We see the two *trilithons* on the wings or sides of the *adytum*, are set almost in a strait line, one of another; when in a hexagon form, they ought to make a considerable angle. If you examine them trigonometrically, the true angle of an hexagon is 120 degrees, but here is an angle of near 150. And by making it an hexagon, he supposes one *trilithon* entirely gone, *that* nearest the grand entrance, when there is not the least appearance that ever there were such stones there. No cavity in the earth, no stump or fragment visible, nor is it easy to imagine, how 3 stones of so vast a bulk could have been clean carried away, either whole or in pieces. There is no room for them to have been carried away whole, no traces of their having been thrown down, broke in pieces and so carried away. This outer side of the work being the most perfect of the whole. Of the ruins of the other *trilithons*, there is not the least part wanting. What has been thrown down and broke, remains upon the spot. But this *trilithon* in dispute, must needs have been spirited away, by nothing less than Merlin's magic, which erected it, as the monks fable. Besides, if it were still standing, it would be very far from making this adytum a regular hexagon, to which he has accommodated his *peripteros* scheme: p. 87. Further, granting it was a regular hexagon, it would be very far from corresponding with that scheme, or have the least appearance, of its being taken from such a one. For our editor there, has converted the cell quite from the nature of that at *Stonehenge*. He has made the upper end of his cell at the letter H opposite to the grand entrance G, not a *trilithon* as it is notoriously at *Stonehenge*, but an angular interval between 2 *trilithons*. It is not the side of the figure, but the angle. Whereas it is most notorious at *Stonehenge*, that the upper end of the *adytum* opposite to the grand entrance, and to the whole length of the avenue and entrance between it and the area, is a *trilithon*; not an angle or interval. And that *trilithon* is exceeding stately, tho' in ruins, one of the upright stones being fallen, the other leaning. So that here, we have the cell converted full a 6th part of the whole compass, from its true and original situation, and so in all the schemes of Mr. *Webb's* book, not one excepted. In that, for instance, *Scheme* I, p. 56, the high altar is plac'd at D not against a *trilithon*, as it ought to be, opposite to the grand entrance in the front of the temple, and to the (only) entrance below, into the *area*, but against an angle between two. If then you suppose that hexagon remov'd back a 6th part, so as that a *trilithon* be set behind the high altar, as it is really in the thing its self, and upon the principal diameter of the whole work: then this absurd consequence follows, that the opposite *trilithon* of the cell stands in the very midst of the entrance into the cell, upon the same principal ground-line or diameter of the work, and quite obstructs the view and entrance into it. It is altogether as ridiculous, as if a dead wall was built under St. Paul's organ-loft, which is and ought to be the chief entrance into the choir. Besides, by *Webb's* ground-plots and uprights, it seems as if, when you entered this *adytum*, there were 3 *trilithons* on the right, and 3 on the left, whereas it is most obvious, there are but two on the right, and two on the left; when you advance into it, the orderly way, from the north-east grand entrance of the avenue; which he himself p. 55. owns to be the principal. But I am tired of so ungrateful a task, which necessity alone could have extorted from me.

# CHAP. V.

*Of the cell or* adytum *of* Stonehenge. *Of the* Surgeons *amphitheater*, London.

Disputations become cloisters and porticoe's. Let us now with minds free from passion, enter the *adytum* with an intent to find out its true figure, to examine what it really was, and what it is. And that may easily be done, because (as I said before) as to the *trilithons* of which it is chiefly compos'd, they are all remaining. Not a bit is lost, but what mischievous and silly people knock off with hammers, to see whether, as the wretched vulgar notion would have it, the stones be factitious is a design of it, which I made sitting in the center of the grand entrance in the inner circle. This point is properly the door-way or entrance into the *adytum*, as a wicket or little door, whilst the jambs of the hithermost *trilithons* present themselves, as the greater door, of above 40 feet wide, 25 cubits. I observe in the old *Greek* story, many footsteps of the primitive patriarchal way left in their sacred structures, which are parallels to this work before us, and others of our Druids. For instance, *Pausanias in atticis* speaks of a temple dedicate to *Venus*, in the front of which, is a wall (as he calls it) built of rude stones. Nevertheless he concludes it to be a very famous work. One may very well imagine, this wall of rude stones is the remnant of some such old work as ours, left for the sacred regard the people had to it, even after art was risen to great height, together with superstition and idolatry. For that the most ancient *Greeks* had very little of idolatry, any more than our Druids, I shall show when I discourse on that head. Again: the more sacred part of the temple at *Hierapolis* answering to our *Adytum*, had no door, tho' none enter'd therein but the chief priests. *Lucian de deâ Syria.* I suppose it was in imitation of the ancient usage, without doors to shut or open, as our temple here. For the ancients thought it wrong, to confine the deity, as it were, within any cover'd place: 'till *Moses,* by God's direction, made a tabernacle cover'd with skins, which was to adumbrate the Messiah Son of God, who was to be cloathed with our nature. And *Solomon's* temple was built in imitation of this tabernacle. But before that, the ancients meant no more by temples, or altars, as they were first call'd, than a certain known and conspicuous place, ornamented in a particular manner, that should mark out a *kebla,* or a place towards which we are to address the Deity, and that for uniformity sake. As the *Turks* and *Arabians* do now, who are the descendants of *Ishmael,* and had this custom from *Abraham.* Tho' the supreme Being be omnipresent, yet for our convenience, where time, place, and such kind of circumstances are necessary to a public action, he would have, as it were, the place of his presence made notorious. As in the *Jewish* dispensation he did in a most extraordinary manner, by the *shechinah.* And from *Solomon's* temple, all the rest of the world borrow'd the fashion of temples, properly so call'd, built magnificently and with roofs. For the sacred houses mention'd in scripture before then, were only little chapels, shrines, like our Druids *kistvaens,* which sometime they carried about in a cart, sometime were fix'd in cities, for publick use; as *Beth Dagon,* and the like. These were but *kistvaens* improv'd, niches turn'd into sacella, in imitation of two or three stones in *Abraham's* altars, which we may well call the *kebla,* and find many of them among our Druid antiquities.

The cell is form'd by a radius of 12 cubits and a half, from the two centers *a* and *b,* as to the inward curve; the outward takes a radius of 15 cubits; for these stones are two cubits and a half thick. The two circles are turn'd into an oval, by a radius of 30 cubits, (after the usual manner) set in the two centers *c* and *d,* where the two circles intersect. The former centers are 12 cubits and a half distant from each other, the length of the radius. The same oval is obtain'd by a string of 60 cubits, the ends ty'd together, and turn'd round upon two centers, according to the gardiners method. An oval form'd as this is, upon two centers coinciding with each other's circumference; or, which is the same thing, whose centers are distant from each other the length of their radius, is most natural and most beautiful, being the shape of an egg. Most probably these religious philosophers had a meaning, in thus including an egg-like figure, within a circle, more than mere affectation of variety. Whatever that was, we may reasonably conclude, that from the method in antiquity, of making the *kebla* of a curved figure, the christians borrowed theirs of turning the east end of their churches in that manner; and that the Druids in the work before us, have produc'd the noblest *kistvaen* or *kebla* that is known.

My purpose in drawing many prickt lines upon the plate, is not difficult to be understood. Nor does it require particular explanations. To avoid affectation or tediousness, I leave them to the readers amusement: only observe, that Mr. *Webb's* equilateral triangles have no hand in forming the cell. The intent of it is very distant from a regular polygon. But that it is incomparably more beautiful; than such a one would have render'd it. It is as a magnificent niche 27 cubits long, and as much broad, measuring in the widest place.

This part is call'd Σηκος or *concha templi* and *adytum*, into which, we may suppose, none but the upper order of priests, together with the high-priest, were commonly to enter, during the time of ministration, in religious rites. We may imagine the beauty of the appearance here upon those occasions, when an innumerable company of the Druids assisted, all in white surplices. The center of the excentricity of this oval is but three cubits nearer the entrance, than the center of the whole work. And they have cut off but one *trilithon*, which they make the opening of the *adytum*; meeting the eye to great advantage, from the grand entrance. By the aforesaid contrivance, there is left a space of five cubits between the jambs of the opening of the *adytum*, and the inner circle in front, just the same as is between the inner and outer circle. The inner circle there performing the office of *cancelli* to it, as we observ'd before. If a choir of this form was put in practice, and executed by a masterly hand, it would have a very extraordinary effect, and perhaps excel the too similar concave of a cupola.

Plate 13. Prospect of STONEHENGE from the Southwest

Our Druids had undoubtedly such a notion, in placing this within a circle. And for the sake of this, they turn'd the two circles into a smaller species of an ellipsis.

There's a Druid antiquity like our *adytum* in shape, call'd *Eglwys Glominog*, on the top of *Arennig vaur* in *Lhanykil* parish, *Merionydhshire*, but made of a continued wall. The ancients thought the world of an egg-like shape, and as the world is the temple of the Deity, they judg'd it proper to form their temples, so as to have a resemblance thereto. The ancient hieroglyphic of the Deity is a circle, and I have reason to believe it more ancient than the flood. *Plato*, who learnt much from the ancestors of our Druids, says in *Diogenes Laertius*, that God is spherical, which he must mean hieroglyphically. So our Druids, as well as he, may mean the infinity of nature in the Deity, who made the world, by this scheme of *Stonehenge*; at least they understand by the circle, the seat and residence of the Deity, the heavens, which include all things.

It seems to me, that *Inigo Jones* from this *adytum* projected the plan of the Surgeons theatre in *London*, a fabric for seeing and hearing much admired by all good judges. And which my Lord *Burlington*, out of a spirit truly noble, and a great love for the architect's memory, has lately repair'd, with his own charges and excellent skill. I find the *Surgeons* theatre (or rather amphitheatre) is form'd from the same proportion as our *adytum*, the transverse and conjugate diameters being as 4 to 3, *viz.* 40 foot and 30 foot. And this appears to me a strong presumption, that *Inigo Jones* did not make the ground-plot of *Stonehenge*, publish'd under his name. The *Surgeons* amphitheatre is a good deal less than our cell.

Such is the noble and easy geometry of the *adytum* of *Stonehenge*. The stones that compote it, are really stupendous, their height, breadths and thickness are enormous, and to see so many of them plac'd together, in a nice and critical figure, with exactness; to consider, as it were, not a pillar of one stone, but a whole wall, a side, an end of a temple of one stone; to view them curiously, creates such a motion in the mind, which words can't express. One very remarkable particular in the construction of this *adytum*, has escaped all observers: which is this. As this part is compos'd of *trilithons* (as I before call them) sett two and two on each side, and one right before; they rise in height and beauty of the stones, from the lower end of the *adytum*, to the upper end. My meaning is this. The two hithermost *trilithons* corresponding, or those next the grand entrance, on the right hand, and on the left are exceeded in height, by the two next in order; and those are exceeded by the *trilithon* behind the altar, in the upper end of this choir. So that in laying down the measures of the parts, that compose this place, the reader must be content to take my word. Mr. *Webb's* measures cannot be precise in all of them, seeing he knew nothing of this particular; and that his notion of an hexagon, is contradicted by it, as well as by fact. "He says p. 60. the stones of the greater hexagon seven foot and a half in breadth, three foot nine inches thick, and twenty foot high, each stone having one tenon in the middle." His measure of seven foot and a half in breadth, only shews the vastness of the stones, it is no precise measure, for the founders regarded not any preciseness in their breadth: because two together were design'd to make a *compages*, whereon to set the impost, and this I call a *trilithon*. Each *trilithon* stands by its self, independant of its neighbour, not as the stones and imposts of the outer circle, link'd together in a continued *corona*, by the imposts carried quite round. Indeed the breadth of a stone at bottom is seven feet and a half, which is 4 cubits and a half. Two stones therefore amount to nine cubits, and there is a cubit of interval between them, making in the whole ten cubits. But they were not careful of the particulars, only of the whole, in one of these *compages* or *trilithons*.

The stones of the cell are made to diminish very much, towards the top, most apparently with a design, to take off from their weight, and render them what we call top-heavy, in a less degree. Hence the interval between the two upright stones of the *compages* widens so much upwards. This must certainly contribute very much, to their stability. In assigning 20 foot for their height, Mr. *Webb* has well taken the *medium*. A very small matter more than 20 feet makes exactly

12 cubits of the *Hebrews, Egyptians* and Druids. The reader remembers the proportion I assign'd between the *English* foot and this cubit. 20 inches and 4/5 make a cubit, therefore 20 feet and 4/5 make 12 cubits. The true case as to the height of the *trilithons*, is thus respectively, and which may be seen in with the harmony and symmetry, in the proportion of the whole. We may observe their gradual rising in height, all from the same base, like pillars of higher orders and more diameters. But the intelligent reader must needs see, that our founders never had sight of *Greek* or *Roman* pillars, and never pretended to imitate them, or take any one idea from them. And of these three different orders or degrees of altitude, in these *trilithons*, one exceeds the other by a cubit. So that their heights respectively are 13 cubits, 14. cubits, 15 cubits.

The imposts of these *trilithons* are all of the same height. Mr. *Webb* p. 61. "informs us, the architrave lying on the top of the great stones of the hexagon and mortaised also into them sixteen foot long, 3 foot 9 inches broad, 3 foot 4 inches high." Mr. *Webb*'s 16 foot long, is too scanty, it amounting to 9 cubits and 2 palms, but the intent of the founders was to make these imposts equal both in length and breadth to the foundation of the upright stones that supports them, I mean the two stones at bottom, the sustaining part of the *compages*, which in its whole breadth makes 10 cubits; and 10 cubits long the imposts are to be assign'd. Most certainly whoever undertake to measure them, whether from those fallen on the ground, or still in their proper place, will be apt to fail in giving them just length. Both because 1. 'tis observable that these imposts are form'd somewhat broader upwards, than in their bottom part; but this may not be taken notice of by every one. This was done very judiciously upon an optical principle, which it is plain the founders were aware of. For a stone of so considerable an elevation, by this means only,

72

presents its whole face in view. Therefore they that measure it at bottom will not take its true length. 2. If they take the dimension, either from a stone still in its proper place, or from one fallen down, they will be very liable to shorten the measure. For in the first case, the upper edge of these imposts, must needs have suffer'd from the weather, in so elevated an exposure, thro' the space of 2000 years. It is very apparent they have suffered not a little. Large and deep furrows of age are visible all around them. But if they measure those fallen, they must well imagine such have doubly suffered, from weather, and from the people every day diminishing all corners and edges, to carry pieces away with them. So that in this cafe, analogy and symmetry only can supply these defects. Thus we found before, that the breadth of the imposts of the outer circle is equal to their ichnographical breadth: so it is here, being to cubits. Besides, the outer face of these imposts is longer than the inner, as being in the larger circle. Therefore ten cubits is to be understood their medium measure.

Mr. *Webb* gives it as a general measure, that they are 3 foot 9 inches broad. He has before told us, the uprights which support them were 3 foot 9 thick; take that twice, it makes 7 foot and a half, which he assigns for the breadth, of the uprights. This is all just within a trifle, and it is not expected that he who was not aware of the cubit, by which these works were made, should do it with greater accuracy. The truth of the whole is this: *Webb's* 7 foot and half is 4 cubits and a half, as we said before; the half of it is 3 foot 9, and a very little more. But this must be taken for the least breadth of the imposts, that at the ends.

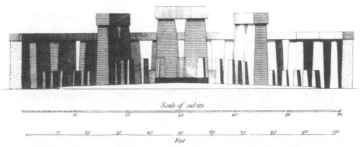

Plate 14. The orthographical Section of Stonehenge upon the Cross diameter

For in the middle they are somewhat broader. Tho' the inside faces are strait, yet, as we observ'd, in proper place, of the imposts of the outer circle; so here, they are rounded behind: their outer circumference answering to the great oval upon which they are founded. So likewise their ends are made upon a *radius* of that oval, whence the inner face of the impost is somewhat shorter than the outer, and is another reason why their lengths may easily be taken somewhat too short. I have drawn the imposts in their true shape in the ground-plot. The artifice of the tenons and mortaises of these *trilithons* and their imposts, what conformity they bear to that of the outer circle, is exceedingly pretty, every thing being done truly geometrical, and as would best answer every purpose, from plain and simple principles. In the bottom face of the impost, if divided into three squares, the two mortaises are made in the middle of the two outermost squares. Draw diagonal lines from corner to corner; where they intersect, is the center of the mortaise; which central distance from one to the other, is seven cubits of the Druid measure. Each tenon is a cubit broad upon its longest diameter, for they are of an oval figure. An admirable contrivance,

74

that the imposts should lie firm upon the heads of the uprights, and keep the uprights steady in their places, to strengthen and adorn. We may remark this pretty device, in the management of the tenons and mortaises. Cut an egg across upon its shortest diameter or conjugate; one half thereof represents the shape of the tenons of the outer circle. Cut it across upon its transverse diameter, one half is the shape of the tenons of the *adytum*. 'Tis evident the meaning of it is this. The tenons of the outer circle are higher in proportion, than the others, because the imposts are less and lower than the others, and on both accounts more liable to be disturb'd, either by accident or violence, than the others: therefore more caution is us'd for their preservation. This is an instance of art, noble and simple withal. Mr. *Webb* says the imposts are 3 foot 4 inches high, which is precisely 2 cubits, a sixth part of the height of the *medium* order of *trilithons*; as the imposts of the outer circle are a sixth part of the height of the stones of the outer circle. The medium order of *trilithons* is above 24 foot high, *i.e.* 14 cubits. The lower order is 13 cubits, *viz.* those next the entrance. The upper *trilithon* behind the altar was 15 cubits. Each rising a cubit higher than the other, as we before observ'd.

I promis'd to show the reader what *Stonehenge* is, and what it was. The latter, I presume, is done in the four prints being geometric orthographical sections of the whole work, all necessary ways, such as architects prepare in design, when they set about a building. 'Tis wholly needless to spend many words in explaining them. What the work is, of our *adytum* at present, is shown in the subsequent prints. The one shows the front of the temple when in perfection, the other as now in ruins. Particularly they explain, what I spoke of, as to the orderly rising of the *trilithons* in height, one above another, from the lower end to the upper end of the *adytum*. 'Tis an oblique prospect of it, from the entrance.

The quantity of the solid is well adjusted, in proportioning the stone-work of this *adytum*, to the intervals upon the ichnography. Each *trilithon* is 10 cubits, and each interval about 6. The jambs, or *vacuum* of the entry expand themselves to 25 cubits, which is about 43 feet. From which measure my Lord *Pembroke* demonstrated the falsity of *Webb*'s hexagonal scheme, when his Lordship first did me the honour to discourse about *Stonehenge*. In Mr. *Webb*'s designs, we find two jambs (taking one *trilithon* away) expand but little above 31 feet, by his own scales. Tho' I don't pretend, but that some of my foregoing measures, may here and there possibly vary a little, upon a very strict trial, and where proper judgment is not us'd, because the stones in some parts may protuberate, or great parts of them may have fallen off; yet 10 foot difference from truth cannot be allow'd of. I observe the inside of that upright stone, which makes the northern jamb of the chief entrance of the outer circle. A very great piece is fallen off towards the top, which discovers its tenon and the mortaise of the impost above it. And in the management of such prodigious stones as these are, fix'd in the ground, and ramm'd too like posts: 'tis not to be wonder'd at, if by chance we find some little variation. Tho' for my own part, I observ'd none; rather wonder'd, how it was possible for them, without lewices and the like devices, to set them in their places to such preciseness. And the reader, whole mind has receiv'd no prepossession, cannot but be abundantly satisfy'd, that the multitude of measures I have given from Mr. *Webb*'s own account, are perfectly agreeable to the scale of cubits, deduc'd from works of the *Egyptians* and others: and that in round and full numbers, not trifling fractions. If we collate the numbers given, with the *Roman* scale, the measures appear very ridiculous and without design; and that is a sure way of confuting the opinion, of its being a *Roman* work. But as these stones are generally rough, and by time must suffer in all dimensions, 'tis not practical to take their true measure, without necessary judgment, and relation had to symmetry.

Of these greater stones of the *adytum*, as I observed before, there are none wanting. They are all on the spot, 10 upright stones, 5 cornishes. The *trilithon* first on the left hand is entire *in situ*, but vastly decay'd, especially the cornish. There are such deep holes corroded, in some places, that dawn make their nests in them. The next *trilithon* on the left hand, is entire, compos'd of three most beautiful stones. The cornish happen'd to be of a very durable kind of *English* marble, and has not been much impair'd by weather. My Lord *Winchelsea* and myself took a considerable walk on the top of it, but it was a frightful situation. The *trilithon* of the upper end of the adytum, was an extraordinary beauty. But alas through the indiscretion probably, of some body digging there, between them and the altar, the noble impost is dislodg'd from its airy seat, and fallen upon the altar, where its huge bulk lies unfractur'd.

> *Recidit in solidam longo post tempore, terram*
> *Pondus, & exhibuit junctam cum viribus artem.*
> Ovid *Met.*

The two uprights that supported it are the most delicate stones of the whole work. They were, I believe, above 30 foot long, and well chizell'd, finely taper'd and proportion'd in their dimensions. That southward is broke in two, lying upon the altar. The other frill stands entire, but leans upon one of the stones of the inward oval.

> *Jam jam lapsura cadentique*
> *Imminet assimilis----------*

The root-end or unhewn part of both, are rais'd somewhat above ground. We cannot be sure of the true height of this, when it was perfect: but I am sure 15 cubits, which I have assign'd, is the lowest. The next *trilithon, that* toward the west, is intire, except that some of the end of the impost is fallen

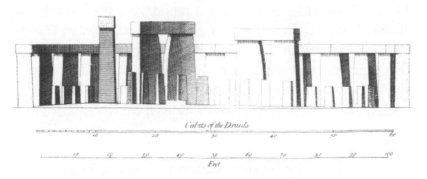

Plate 15. The Orthographic Section of Stonehenge up on the Chief diameter

clean off; and all the upper edge is very much diminish'd by time. As *Lucretius* says,

> --------*Minui rem quamque videmus,*
> *Et quasi longinquo fluere omnia cernimus ævo,*
> *Ex oculisque, vetustatem, subducere nostris.*

The last *trilithon,* that on the right hand of the entrance into the *adytum,* has suffer'd much. The outer upright being the jamb of the entrance, is still standing, the other upright and impost are both fallen forwards into the *adytum,* and broke each into three pieces. I suppose from digging near it. But from one piece of the impost lying look, in the middle, between the jambs of the adytum, Mr. *Webb* in the plan of his ruins of *Stonehenge* (being his 6th *Scheme*) forms the remains of his imaginary 6th *trilithon*, supposing it one of the stones of the inner or lesser hexagon, as he calls it. Yet if this fragment was really a stump of such a stone, as he would have it, still it would not create an hexagonal form of the cell, but stand just in the middle of the entrance, and block it up in a very absurd, unseemly, and incommodious a manner. And nothing can be more certain, than that there never was such a thing in being. That stone of the *trilithon* which is standing, has a cavity in it which two or three persons may sit in, worn by the weather.

*Stonehenge* is compos'd of two circles and two ovals, respectively concentric. At the distance of two cubits inward from the greater oval, describe another lesser oval, on which the stones of the inner oval are to stand: 19 stones in number, at about the central distance of 3 cubits. This lesser oval is to be describ'd by a string and the 2 centers, as before. Or by 2 circles from a 10 cubit *radius*, and the 2 centers *a* and *b*, as of the other before was spoken. Mr. Webb says, p. 60, "the stones of the hexagon within, 2 foot 6 inches in breadth, one foot and a half thick and 8 foot high, in form pyramidal." His two foot and a half is our cubit and half; for the breadth of these stones; being but a third of the breadth of the stones of the greater oval. And the interval between stone and stone, the same. Their height is likewise unequal, as the *trilithon*, for they rise in height as nearer the upper end of the *adytum*. Mr. *Webb's* 8 foot assign'd, is a good *medium* measure, for it is just 4 cubits and 4 palms, the third part of the height of the *medium trilithon*. From the ruins of those left, we may well suppose, the first next the entrance and lowest were 4 cubits high; the most advanc'd height behind the altar might be five cubits, and perhaps more. The stones are somewhat of what Mr. *Webb* calls a pyramidal form, meaning that of an *Egyptian* obelisk, for they taper a little upwards. They are of a much harder sort than the other stones, as we spoke before, in the lesser circle. The founders provided that their lesser bulk should be compensated in solidity. They were brought somewhere from the west. Of these there are only 6 remaining upright. The stumps of two are left on the south side by the altar. One lies behind the altar, dug up or thrown down, by the fall of that upright there. One or two were thrown down probably, by the fall of the upright of the first *trilithon* on the right hand. A stump of another remains by the upright there, still standing. Their exact measures either as to height, breadth or thickness, cannot well be ascertain'd. For they took such as they could find, best suiting their scantlings, but the stones were better shap'd and taller, as advancing towards the upper end of the cell.

# CHAP. VI.

*Of the number of the stones. Of the altar-stone. Of what has been found in digging, about the temple. A plate of tin of the Druids writing. A plate of gold, supposed to be of the Druids writing.*

THUS have we finished the work, or principal part of this celebrated wonder; properly the temple or sacred structure, as it may be called. Tho' its loftiest crest be compos'd but of one stone, laid upon another. "A work, as Mr. *Webb* says justly, p. 65. built with much art, order and proportion." And it must be own'd, that they who had a notion, that it was an unworthy thing, to pretend to confine the deity in room and space, could not easily invent a grander design than this, for sacred purposes: nor execute it in a more magnificent manner. Here space indeed is mark'd out and defin'd: but with utmost freedom and openness. Here is a *kebla* intimating, but not bounding the presence of the Deity. Here the variety and harmony of four differing circles presents itself continually new, every step we take, with opening and closing light and shade. Which way so ever we look, art and nature make a composition of their highest gusto, create a pleasing astonishment, very apposite to sacred places.

The great oval consists of 10 uprights, the inner with the altar, of 20, the great circle of 30, the inner of 40. to, 20, 30, 40 together, make 100 upright stones. 5 imposts of the great oval, 30 of the great circle, the 2 stones standing upon the bank of the *area*, the stone lying within the entrance of the *area*, and that standing without. There seems to have been another stone lying upon the ground, by the *vallum* of the court, directly opposite to the entrance of the avenue. All added together, make just 140 stones, the number of which *Stonehenge*, a whole temple, is compos'd. Behold the solution of the mighty problem, the magical spell is broke, which has so long perplex'd the vulgar! they think 'tis an ominous thing to count the true number of the stones, and whoever does so, shall certainly die after it. Thus the Druids contented themselves to live in huts and caves: whilst they employ'd many thousands of men, a whole county, to labour at these publick structures, dedicated to the Deity.

Our altar here is laid toward the upper end of the *adytum*, at present flat on the ground, and squeez'd (as it were) into it, by the weight of the ruins upon it. 'Tis a kind of blue coarse marble, such as comes from *Derbyshire*, and laid upon tombs in our churches and church-yards. Thus *Virgil* describes an ancient altar, after the *Etruscan* fashion, and which probably had remain'd from patriarchal times.

> *Ædibus in mediis nudoque sub ætheris axe*
> *Ingens ara fuit.*--------- Æne. II.

*Servius* upon the IIId *Georg.* says, in the middle of a temple was the place of the Deity: the rest was only ornamental. This altar is plac'd a little above the *focus* of the upper end of the ellipsis. Mr. *Webb* says, p. 56. the altar is 4 foot broad, 16 in length. 4 foot is 2 cubits 2 palms, which at four times measures 16 foot. I believe its breadth is 2 cubits 3 palms, *i.e.* 1 and a half: and that its first intended length was 10 cubits, equal to the breadth of the *trilithon* before which it lies. But 'tis very difficult to come at its true length. 'Tis 20 inches thick, a just cubit, and has been squar'd. It lies between the two centers, that of the compasses and that of the string: leaving a convenient space quite round it, no doubt, as much as was necessary for their ministration.

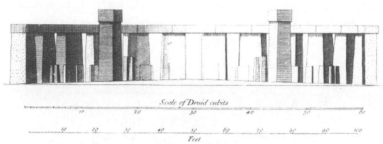

*The Section of Stonehenge looking towards the Entrance.*

Plate 16. The Section of Stonehenge looking towards the Entrance.

Mr. *Webb* says, the heads of oxen, and deer, and other beasts have been found upon digging in and about *Stonehenge*, as divers then living could testify, undoubted reliques of sacrifices, together with much charcoal, meaning wood-ashes. Mr. *Camden* says, mens bones have been found hereabouts. He means in the barrows adjacent, and I saw such thrown out by the rabbets very near the temple. But eternally to be lamented is the loss of that tablet of tin, which was found at this place, in the time of King *Henry* VIII. (the *Æra* of restitution of learning and of pure religion) inscrib'd with many letters, but in so strange a character, that neither Sir *Thomas Elliot* a learned antiquary, nor Mr. *Lilly* master of St. Paul's school, could make any thing out of it. Mr. *Sammes* may be in the right, who judges it to have been *Punic*; I imagine if we call it *Irish*, we shall not err much. No doubt but it was a memorial of the founders, wrote by the Druids: and had it been preserv'd till now, would have been an invaluable curiosity. To make the reader some amends for such a loss, I have given a specimen of supposed Druid writing, out of *Lambecius*'s account of the Emperor's library at *Vienna*. 'Tis wrote on a wry thin plate of gold, with a sharp-pointed in-

83

strument. It was in an urn found at *Vienna*, roll'd up in several cases of other metal, together with funeral *exuviæ*. It was thought by the curious, one of those epistles, which the *Celtic* people were wont to send to their friends in the other world. So certain a hope of a future pate had the Druids infus'd into them. The reader may divert himself with endeavouring to explain it. The writing upon plates of gold or tin is exceeding ancient, as we see in *Job* xix. 24.

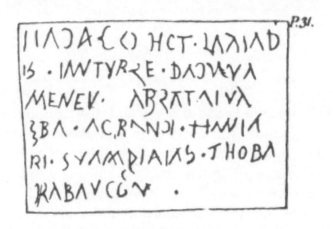

Plutarch in his pamphlet *de dæmonio Socratis* tells a similar story. "About the time of *Agesilaus*, they found a brazen tablet in the sepulchre of *Ahemena* at *Thebes*, wrote in characters unknown, but seem'd to be *Egyptian. Chonuphis*, the most learned of the Egyptian prophets then, being consulted upon it, confirm'd it, and said it was wrote about the time of *Hercules* and *Proteas* king in Egypt. *Tzetzes*, chil. 2. hist. 44. mentions Proteus a king in lower Egypt by the sea side, pretends he was son of *Neptune* and *Phœnicia*, throwing him up thereby to very ancient times, those of the first famous navigators, our *Hercules* and the *Phœnicians*. He is said to have lived in the island afterward call'd *Pharos*, from the watchtower there erected. Here *Homer* sings, that *Proteus* diverts himself with his *phocæ* or sea-calves, most undoubtedly his ships. But at that time of day, every thing new and strange was told by the *Greeks* in a mythologic way.

In the year 1635, as they were plowing by the barrows about *Normanton* ditch, they found a large quantity of excellent pewter, as much as they sold at a low price for 5*l*. says Mr. *Aubry* in his manuscript collections, relating to antiquities of this sort. There are several of these ditches, being very small in breadth, which run across the downs. I take them for boundaries of hundreds of parishes, *&c*. I suspect this too was a tablet with an inscription on it, but falling into the hands of the countrymen, they could no more discern the writing, than interpret it. No doubt but this was some of the old *British stanum*, which the *Tyrian Hercules*, sirnam'd *Melcarthus*, first brought *ex Cassiteride insula*, or *Britain*. Which *Hercules* liv'd in *Abraham*'s time, or soon after.

Mr. *Webb* tells us, the Duke of *Buckingham* dug about *Stonehenge:* I fear much to the prejudice of the work. He himself did the like, and found what he imagin'd was the cover of a *thuribulum*. He would have done well to have given us a drawing of it. But whatever it was, vases of incense, oil, slower, salt, wine and holy water, were used by all nations in their religious ceremonies.

Mr. *Thomas Hayward*, late owner of *Stonehenge*, dug about it, as he acquainted Lord *Winchelsea* and myself. He found heads of oxen and other beasts bones, and nothing else. In 1724. when I was there, *Richard Hayns* an old man of *Ambresbury*, whom I employed to dig for me in the barrows, found some little worn-out *Roman* coins at *Stonehenge*, among the earth rooted up by the rabbets. He sold one of them for half a crown, to Mr. *Merril* of *Golden Square*, who came thither whilst I was at the place. The year before, *Hayns* was one of the workmen employ'd by Lord *Carlton* to dig clay on *Harra-don* hill, east of *Ambresbury*, where they found many *Roman* coins, which I saw. I suspect he pretended to find those at *Stonehenge*, only for sake of the reward. My friend the late Dr. *Harwood* of *Doctors-Commons* told me, he was once at *Stonehenge* with such sort of *Roman* coins in his pockets, and that one of his companions would have persuaded him, to throw some of them into the rabbit-holes: but the Doctor was more ingenuous. Nevertheless were never so many such coins found in *Stonehenge*, they would prove nothing more, than that the work was in being, when the *Romans* were here; and which we are assured of already. I have a brass coin given me by *John Collins* Esq; collector of the excise at *Stamford*. The heads of *Julius* and *Augustus* averse: the reverse a crocodile, palm-branch and garland. COL. NEM. the colony of Nemausus in France. It was found upon *Salisbury* plain; and might be lost there before the *Roman* conquest of *Britain* under *Claudius*, by people of *France* coming hither; or in after-ages: no matter which.

*July* 5 1723. By Lord *Pembroke*'s direction, I dug on the inside of the altar about the middle: 4 foot along the edge of the stone, 6 foot forward toward the middle of the *adytum*. At a foot deep, we came to the solid chalk mix'd with flints, which had never been stir'd. The altar was exactly a cubit thick, 20 inches and 4/5; but broken in two or three pieces by the ponderous masses of the impost, and one upright stone of that *trilithon* which stood at the upper end of the *adytum*, being fallen upon it. Hence appears the commodiousness of the foundation for this huge work. They dug holes in the solid chalk, which would of itself keep up the stones, as firm as is a wall was built round them. And no doubt but they ramm'd up the interstices with flints. But I had too much regard to the work, to dig any where near the stones. I took up an oxe's tooth, above ground, without the *adytum* on the right hand of the lowermost *trilithon*, north-ward. And this is all the account, of what has been found by digging at *Stonehenge*, which I can give.

Plate 17. An inward View of Stonehenge. Aug. 1722 from the north.

# CHAP. VII.

*Of the area round Stonehenge. The bowing stones. The manner of sacrificing.*

OF the court round the temple of *Stonehenge*, somewhat is said already and of the two stones standing within the *vallum*: and of the two cavities remarkable, which have some correspondency therewith. I supposed, they were places, where two great vases of water stood, for the service of the temple, when they perform'd religious rites here. And I endeavour'd to illustrate it by a coin of the city *Heliopolis*. 60 cubits is the diameter of *Stonehenge*, 60 more reaches the inner edge of the circular ditch of the court. The ditch originally was near 30 cubits broad, but thro' long tract of time, and the infinity of coaches, horses, &c. coming every day to see the place, 'tis levell'd very much. The intire diameter of the court, reaching to the outward verge of the ditch, is 4 times 60 cubits, which is about 410 foot. The five outer circles of the ditch are struck with a radius of 80, 90, 100, 110, 120 cubits.

Just upon the inner verge of the ditch, at the entrance from the avenue, lies a very large stone, at present flat on the ground. Mr. *Webb*, p. 57. pretends to give us the measure of it, confounding it with the other two before-mention'd to be within the *vallum*, to which they have no relation, no similarity in proportion. This is to favour his notion of three entrances of the *area*, dependant upon his hypothesis of equilateral triangles. He there tells us at the letter F, "the parallel stones on the inside of the trench were four foot broad and three foot thick; but they lie so broken and ruin'd by time, that their proportion in height cannot be distinguish'd, much less exactly measur'd." Thus he, but 'tis *invita Minervâ*; for all three stones, in all appearance, are as little alter'd from their first size, as any stones in the work. The two stones within the *vallum* are very small stones, and ever were so. The one stands; the other leans a little, probably from some idle people digging about it. This stone at the entrance is a very great one, near as big as any one of the whole work, and seems too as little alter'd from its original form: only thrown down perhaps by the like foolish curiosity of digging near it. Instead of *Webb*'s four foot broad, it's near seven: but to speak in the Druid measure, four cubits. It is at present above 20 feet long. If it stood originally, and a little leaning, it was one of those stones which the *Welsh* call *crwm lechen*, or bowing-stones. However, Mr. *Webb* must falsify the truth very much, in making this and the two former any thing alike in dimension, situation and use. But he does so, much more in the next, which is doubtless a *crwm leche*, still standing in its original posture and place in the avenue. 'Tis of much the like dimension as the other, tho' not so shapely, and stands in like manner on the left hand, or south, of the middle line, of the length of the avenue. I surmise, the Druids consider'd the propriety of making the other a little more shapely than this, because within the *area*, and nearer the sacred fabric. There is the distance of 119 feet between them, to speak properly, 80 cubits. This interval Mr. *Webb* contracts to about 43 foot, and supposes there was another stone to answer it on the right hand, as also another to answer that on the inside the ditch. And he supposes the like of those before-mention'd, both within and without the ditch, at his two

89

fancy'd entrances. But of these, there is *nec vola nec vestigium*, and I dare say, never was. This stone has a hole in it, which is observable of like stones, set thus near our like temples: as we shall see in the progress of this work. The stone is of 24 foot in circumference, 16 high above ground, 9 broad, 6 thick. The use of it I can't certainly tell; but I am inclin'd to think, that as part of the religious worship in old patriarchal times, consisted in a solemn adoration, or three silent bowings: the first bowing might be perform'd at this stone, just without the ditch, the second perhaps at the next stone, just within the ditch. Then they turn'd by that stone to the left hand, as the manner was, in a procession round the temple, both the priests and animals for sacrifice. At those two stones and water-vases, probably there were some washings, lustrations, or sprinklings with holy water, and other ceremonies, which I don't pretend to ascertain. Then upon the entry into the temple, perhaps they made the third bow, as in presence of the Deity. After this, in the *court*, we may suppose the priests prepar'd the hecatombs and customary sacrifices. If that great stone just within the ditch, always lay, as it does now, flat on the ground, and *in situ*, (which I am not unwilling to believe) then, I apprehend, it was a table for dressing the victims. *Ezekiel*, in describing the temple of *Jerusalem*, speaks of such in the entry, xl. 30, 40, 41, 42, 43.

'Tis just to think, the ancient form of sacrificing here, like that of the *Romans*, *Greeks* or elder nations, was pretty much the same as that among the *Jews*, and that as in patriarchal times; and in short, no other than the original practice of mankind, since the first institution of sacrifices, at the fall. Therefore we shall subjoin it from *Homer*'s description, in *Iliad* I. It quadrates extremely well, in all appearance, with the place and temple before us.

Straightway in haste, a chosen hecatomb
To God, prepar'd, the well-built altar round,
They place in order. Then their hands they wash,
And take the salted meal. Aloud the priest,
With hands uplifted, for the assembly prays.
After the prayers, they wav'd the salted meal,
And then retiring slay the animals.
The skins being stript, they cut off both the thighs,
And cover them with cawl; first offer'd crude.
The priest then burns a part on plates,
In another place he adds, thereon red wine,
Libation pour'd. The ministring young men
Stand by him, with their five-fold spits in hand.
But when the thighs are burnt, out of the rest
Entrails and flesh, harslets and stakes they make,
Upon the spits transfixt. Then roasted well
They set all forth. After the duty done;
A feast they next prepare. Plenty of food
Distributed around, chearful repast.
Banquet being o're, the youths huge goblets crown,
And fill to all in cups. Then sacred hymns
Sung to the Deity, conclude the day.
With choice cloven bits of wood,
Without leaves--------------------

These are most ancient rites, symbolical of the purity of the sacrifice of the *Messiah*, pointed at by, and deriv'd from the *Mosaic* dispensation, where every thing of sacred purpose was to be perfect.

Thus much is sufficient to give the reader an idea of the ancient manner of sacrificing, such, no doubt as was practis'd at this very place entirely the *Hebrew* rite. I suppose only the priests and chief personages came within the *area*, who made the procession with the sacrifices along the avenue. The multitude kept without, on foot or in their chariots.

Plate 18. A direct view of the Remains of the adytum of Stonehenge

# CHAP. VIII.

*Of the Avenue to* Stonehenge.

THE Avenue of *Stonehenge* was never observ'd by any who have wrote of it, tho' a very elegant part of it, and very apparent. It answers, as we have said before now, to the principal line of the whole work, the northeast, where abouts the sun rises, when the days are longest. *Plutarch* in the life of *Numa* says, the ancients observ'd the rule of setting their temples, with the front to meet the rising sun. *Promachidas* of *Heracleum*, and *Dionysius Thrax* take notice of the same thing. And this was done in imitation of the *Mosaic* tabernacle and *Solomon*'s temple: probably a patriarchal rite. This avenue extends itself, somewhat more than 1700 feet, in a strait line, down to the bottom of the valley, with a delicate descent. I observe the earth of the ditches is thrown inward, and seemingly some turf on both sides, thrown upon the avenue: to raise it a little above the level of the downs. The two ditches continue perfectly parallel to the bottom, 40 cubits asunder. About midway, there is a pretty depressure, natural, which diversifies it agreeably. *Stonehenge*, I said, is not on the highest part of the hill. I found, the reason, why the Druids set it just where it is; because it is precisely 1000 cubits from the bottom to the entrance of the *area*. When I began my inquiries into this noble work, I thought it terminated here, and Mr. *Roger Gale* and myself measur'd it so far with a chain. Another year, I found it extended itself much farther. For at the bottom of the valley, it divides into two branches. The eastern branch goes a long way hence, directly east pointing to an ancient ford of the river *Avon*, called *Radfin*, and beyond that the visto of it bears directly to *Harradon* hill beyond the river. The western branch, from this termination at the bottom of the hill 1000 cubits from the work at *Stonehenge*, as we said, goes off with a similar sweep at first; but then it does not throw itself into a strait line immediately, as the former, but continues curving along the bottom of the hill, till it meets, what I call, the *cursus*. This likewise is a new unobserv'd curiosity belonging to this work, and very much enlarges the idea we ought to entertain, of the magnificence and prodigious extent of the thing. The temple which we have been hitherto describing, considerable indeed as it really is, in itself; yet now appears as a small part of the whole. I shall therefore describe all these parts separately, to render them more intelligible: and then show their connection, and what relation they have, to one another, as well as I can. But it is not easy to enter at once, into the exceeding greatness of thought, which these people had, who founded it; bringing in all the adjacent country, the whole of nature hereabouts, to contribute its part to the work. Therefore I shall discourse of it backward and forward; first going from *Stonehenge* to its termination, or more properly its beginning, and then return again. Explaining all the way, what is its present condition, and what, 'tis reasonable to suppose, was its original, when the Druids made their first design. This together with the several views I have drawn of it, will give us nearly as good a notion of the whole, as we can at this day expect, and perhaps preserve the memory of it hereafter, when the traces of this mighty work are obliterated with the plough, which it is to be fear'd, will be its fate. That instrument gaining ground too much, upon the ancient and innocent pastoritial life; hereabouts, and everywhere else in *England:* and by destructive inclosures beggars and depopulates the country.

At the bottom of the valley, and the end of the strait part of *Stonehenge.* avenue, 100 cubits from *Stonehenge*, as we said, the eastern wing of the avenue turns off to the right, with a circular sweep, and then in a strait line proceeds eastward up the hill. It goes just between those two most conspicuous groups of barrows, crowning the ridg of that hill eastward of *Stonehenge*; between it and *Vespasian's* camp, separated from them both by a deep valley on each side. These two groups of barrows are called generally the seven king's graves, each. I call that most northerly, the old seven kings graves, for there are really 7, tho' but 6 most apparent; they are all set at greater distance, all broader, flatter, and as it is most reasonable to suppose, older than the other. The other are set closer together, of a more elegantly turn'd figure, campaniform, and in all appearance, much later than the former. Therefore I call these, being southward and directly between *Stonehenge* and the town of *Ambresbury*, the new seven kings barrows. Of the seven old, the most northerly one and probably the oldest, is exceeding flat and as it were, almost sunk into the earth with age; so that it is scarce visible at a distance. The avenue runs up to the top of the hill, just between them: and they make as it were wings to it, and I believe were design'd as such, when set there. When the avenue first turns off in the valley, it is much obscur'd by the wheels of carriages going over it, for a great way together: for this is the road to *Lavington*. Nevertheless a curious eye, without difficulty, sees all the traces of it sufficiently, till it is got higher up the easy ascent of the hill, and out of the common road. Then it is very apparent and consists of the two little ditches as before, (when coming directly from *Stonehenge*) exactly parallel, and still 40 cubits asunder. And it is made with the same degree of variation, or about 6 degrees southward from the true east point. So that it is evident again, the Druids intended it should go full east, but their compass by which they set it, varied so much at that time, according to my opinion of the matter. To perpetuate the mark of it as much as I can: I measured the distance of it from the southern ditch thereof, to the ditch of the nearest *i.e.* most northerly of the new 7 kings barrows, and when in the right line of those 7 barrows: it is 257 feet. I know not whether there was any design in it, but it is exactly 150 cubits. From the northern ditch of the avenue here, to the nearest of the old seven kings barrows, is 350 foot; which is exactly 200 cubits.

Whilst we are here upon the elevation of this hill, between these two groups of barrows, 'tis 2700 feet from the beginning of this wing of the avenue at the bottom of the valley, where it commences. It still continues in the very same direction eastward, till unfortunately broke off by the plow'd ground, 300 feet from hence. This plow'd ground continues for a mile together, as far as the river's side at *Ambersbury*. So that 'tis impossible to trace it any farther. The first plow'd field, that southward, is Mr. *Hayward*'s; the other is TAB. XXVII. of a different estate, call'd *Countess-farm*. And the plowing of these two go on at right angles one of another. That piece on the north side of the avenue, of the latter tenure, goes along the line of the avenue, is long and narrow, and has (as usual with greedy farmers) encroach'd upon and swallow'd up so much of the length of the avenue. And that amounts to 750 feet more in length, which must certainly be added to the avenue. This is all along the eastern declivity of the hill we are upon, *that* of the twice seven kings graves, and reaches near the bottom of the valley, between it and the hill whereon stands *Vespasian*'s camp. Now reason and the judgment I have got in conversing with works of this kind, tell me, the founders would never begin this avenue at the bottom of a valley, but rather on a conspicuous height, which is visible from a great distance of country round. We must suppose the intent of the avenue was to direct the religious procession to the temple; and that at the beginning of it, they made sires early in the morning of that day, when they held their grand festivals, to give notice to all the adjacent country. Therefore when we cross this valley still eastward, with the former direction of the compass, and mount that next hill, whereon stands *Vespasian*'s camp: we find exactly such a place as we could with, and extremely suitable to that purpose. For it commands a very extensive prospect both

Inward View of Stonehenge from the high altar. Aug. 1722.

upwards and downwards of the river, and on the other side of it, for many miles; all about that part of the country where it is highly reasonable to think the old *Britons* liv'd, who frequented this temple. This eminence is north of *Vespasian*'s camp, north-west from *Ambresbury* church. Here is a very large scene of the country taken in. It has a fine gentle rise for half a mile and more, even quite from the ford at *Radfin*. You see the most delightful river *Avon* flank'd with villages on both sides, from almost as far as new *Sarum*, and then to the head of it, 5 miles off. It was the custom of the Druids to give notice, by fires, of the quarterly days of sacrifice. Thus the Druids in *Ireland* before christianity, us'd to kindle a fire call'd in their language *Tlachdgha*, on *All saints* eve, to perform a general sacrifice: as Mr. *Llwyd* mentions in his *Irish* dictionary. Mr. *Toland* speaks of others too. I observ'd there has been a bank across the bottom of the valley, for the more easy passage of the religious ceremony, and this much corroborates my conjecture of the avenue reaching hither.

I am apt to believe from the conformity I have observ'd in these works, that there was a *sacellum* or little temple here upon this hill, where the avenue began. We suppose this might easily be destroy'd when they began to plow here, being so near the town. I have found several of these kind of large stones, either travelling to *Stonehenge*, or from it. One as big as any at *Stonehenge*, lies about 3 miles off northward, in *Durington* fields. Another in the water at *Milford*, another at *Fighelden*; they seem to have been carried back to make bridges, mildams or the like, in the river. There is another in the *London* road, east from *Ambresbury*, about a mile from the town. Another in the water at *Bulford*. A stone stands leaning at *Preshute* farm near the church, as big as those at *Stonehenge*. What confirms me in the conjecture that there was a *sacellum* here originally, is, that an innumerable company of barrows on the opposite hill, on the other side of the river coming down *Haradon* and in the line of the avenue seem to regard it; as is usual in these works. For those barrows are not in sight of *Stonehenge* itself, by reason of the interposition of the hill whereon stand the double groups of seven king's graves. And even those two groups seem to regard this little temple as well as the great one, curving that way. The distance from hence to *Stonehenge* is 4000 cubits.

In order to have a just notion of this avenue, it is necessary to go to the neighbouring height of *Haradon* hill, on the other side the river. The largest barrow there, which I call *Hara*'s and which probably gave name to the hill, is in the line of the avenue; the ford of *Radfin* lying between, as we see in the last *Plate*. I stood upon this hill *May* 11. 1724. during the total eclipse of the sun, of which I gave an account in my *Itinerarium*. Here is a most noble view of the work and country about *Stonehenge*. Whoever is upon the spot cannot fail of a great pleasure in it; especially if the sun be low, either after rising or before setting. For by that means the barrows, the only ornaments of these plains, become very visible, the ground beyond them being illuminated by the suns slaunting rays. You see as far as *Clay-hill* beyond *Warminster* 20 miles off. You see the spot of ground on the hill, whereon stands *Vespasian's* camp, where I conjecture the avenue to *Stonehenge* began, and where there was a *sacellum*, as we conceive. From hence to that spot a valley leads very commodiously to *Radfin*, where the original ford was.

This *Radfin-farm* seems to retain its *Celtic* name: meaning a ford or passage for chariots, the old way of carriage here used. *Rhedeg currere, rhedegsain cursitare*, in *Irish reathaim. Fin* in the old *Irish*, is white. It regards the chalky road which went up from the ford. 'Tis a pretty place, seated in a flexure of the river, which from hence seems to bend its arms both ways, to embrace the beginning of the avenue. The place is very warm, shelter'd from all winds, and especially from the north. I am persuaded it was originally a seat of an Archdruid or Druid. See Mr. *Toland* discoursing of the Druids houses, p. 111. The nuns of *Ambresbury* too had a chapel there. The ford is now quite disus'd, because of the bridge by the town's end; and the road of it is foreclos'd by hedgerows of pastures on both sides the lane, leading northwards from *Ambresbury* to north *Wiltshire*. This road lying between *Radfin* and the beginning of *Stonehenge* avenue, is sweetly adorn'd with *viorna*. We are supposed now to stand on the *tumulus* of *Hara*, an old *Irish* royal name, and possibly the king who was coadjutor in founding *Stonehenge*, who lived, it's likely, in the eastern part of *Wiltshire*: for which reason they directed the avenue this way.

*Et nunc servat honos sedem, tuus, ossaque nomen.*

Here are very many barrows upon this side of the hill, all looking toward the sacred work. Hence we survey *Ambres-*

*bury*, *Vespasian*'s camp, and *Stonehenge*, the *cursus*, and little *Ambresbury*. Likewise a very ancient barrow which answers to that of *Vespasian*'s camp, seeming to be plac'd here with some regularity and regard to the *sacellum* at the beginning of the avenue. This is a long barrow, which I suppose the Archdruids who liv'd at *Radfin*, and perhaps the chief person concern'd in projecting the magnificent work. The reader must indulge me the liberty of these kind of conjectures; there is no evidence positive left in such matters of great antiquity. I have some little reason for it, which I shall mention when we speak of the barrows. There is this present use, to affix thereby names to things, that we may talk more intelligibly about them.

We are next to advance down *Haradon*-hill in the same direction, nearer *Radfin*. This valley leads us very gently to the river.

-----*Qua se subducere colles*
*Incipiunt, mollique jugum demittere clivo*
*Usque ad aquam.*-------------- Virg.

This and the two other views give us a good notion of the country on this side. There are seven barrows together, in the road from *Ambresbury* to *Radfin*, one great one and six little ones, which regard the *sacellum*, but cannot possibly to *Stonehenge*. This was a family burying-place probably of some considerable personage, who liv'd at *Ambresbury*. These plates show us too, the avenue marching up the next hill, where the old and new seven kings barrows receive it again, as wings to it. This is shown more distinct where the corn ground has began to encroach upon it. I could scarce forbear the wish,

*Pereat labor irritus anni.*--------------

When you are gone a little farther toward *Stonehenge*, and arriv'd at the top of the hill, if you turn back you have the view presented to you like that beyond A the beginning of the avenue, is *Radfin*, beyond that *Haradon*. The prospect forward, toward *Stonehenge*, is shown. There you see the union of the two wings of the avenue, at the commencement of the strait part of it C. Again, you may observe the nature of the west wing of the avenue, going with a continued curve round the bottom of the hill, till it enters the *Hippodrom* or *cursus*. At a distance you see *Yansbury* camp, thought to be another of *Vespasian*'s. Next you descend into the valley to the union of the wings of the avenue, and ascend the agreeable part

Plate 20. An inward view of Stonehenge from behind ye high Altar looking toward the grand entrance. A little oblique. Aug. 1722.
A the altar

of it, to the temple. Along here went the sacred pomp, How would it delight one to have seen it in its first splendor!

-------*Jam nunc solennes ducere pompas*
*Ad delubra juvat, cæsosque videre juveneos.*          Virg.

I have often admir'd the delicacy of this ascent to the temple. As soon as you mount from the bottom, 'tis level for a great way together: and the whole length o it is a kind of ridge, for it slopes off both ways from it on each side; so that the rain runs off every way. Just about half way there is a depressure, as a pause or foot pace, showing one half of the avenue ascending, the other descending, both magnificent, in the ancient gusto. There was a temple of *Jupiter Labradæus* near *Mylasa* a city of *Caria*, much frequented. The way leading thither was called sacred, and pav'd 60 furlongs, thro' which their procession went. *Philostratus* says, you went to the temple of *Diana* at *Ephesus*, by a stone portico of a *stadium*. *Pausanias in Phocicis* says, the avenue to the temple of *Minerva Cranea* near *Elatea* is ascending, but so gently that it is imperceptible. Again in Chap. X. we read of a pav'd way, to the oracle at *Delphos*. But the natural pavement of our avenue is much finer. I take notice, that *Jupiter Labradæus* was a statue holding a halbard in his hand, which instrument like a *securis* or amazonian ax, was as a scepter to the *Lydian* kings. And apparently our *English* halbard is the very word, with an asperate way of pronunciation prefix'd, *Labrada*. So our Druids carried about a sharp brass instrument which we often find, call'd a celt, (I know not whence) with which they us'd to cut the *Misletoe*, at their great festival in midwinter. I have represented one hanging at our Druids girdle. It was to be put into the slit at the end of his staff, when used. But of this hereafter. Now with the *Poet* in his celebrated *Ode*

-----------------------------*Quibus*
*Mos unde deductus per omne*
*Tempus, Amazonia securi*
*Dextras obarmet, quærere distuli:*
*Nec scire fas est omnia*--------- Horat.

being arriv'd again at *Stonehenge*, from the last print though. small, we may see the beauty of the curve in the outer circle of that work, especially from the avenue, when the eye is below it. We observe the same in the grand front view.

And now we are return'd to the sacred fabric, we will discourse a little upon these temples in general, and so conclude this chapter.

In Macrob. *Saturn*. I. 18. mention is made of a famous round temple in *Thrace*, where they celebrate most magnificent religious rites. It is upon the hill *Zilmissus*. The temple is open at top. I suppose like ours, not a little round hole like as in the *Pantheon*, nor is it a small round *sacellum* like those little round temples at *Rome* to *Romulus*, to *Vesta*, &c. It is not reasonable to think they should build a *Pantheon* in *Thrace*, nor can I understand it otherwise, than that, it was like our *Stonehenge*, and in truth an ancient patriarchal structure of a primitive model. The Deity here worshipp'd was call'd *Sabazius* says he, some make him *Jupiter*, some the sun, some *Bacchus*. These are the first perversions of the *Jehovah* of the *Jews*. In my Judgment, the name *Sabazius* is a corruption of the *Hebrew* name of God באות□ *sabaoth*, *Deus exercituum*, a title that would well suit the warlike *Thracians*. In time Idolatry debased every thing. When they perform'd the religious rites of *Bacchus*, they cried *Evohe*, *Sabbai*, and call'd him *Evius*, *Evan*, *Sabazius*, &c. *Evohe* is a corrupt manner of pronouncing □□□□ *Jehovah*, and this sacred cry is truly no other than what frequently occurs in holy scripture. □□□□ צְבָאוֹת *Jehovah Sabaoth*. He is the king of glory, *Psalm* xxiv. 10. But I have discoursed on this head in my *Paleographia Sacra* N° I. which will be continued.

*Diodorus Siculus* in his Book II. mentions a very eminent temple of a round form, among the *Hyperboreans*, as he calls them, who inhabit an island situate in the ocean over-against *Gaul*, which is not less than *Sicily*. He gives an odd account from thence mix'd with fable, and seemingly some reports of *Stonehenge* itself.

Mr. *Toland* is confident, this hyperborean region is our *Schetland* isles, whence *Abaris* the Druid and hyperborean philosopher, famous in *Grecian* story. Whilst I am writing this, *March* 6. 1739-40. we had an account read before the *Royal Society*, much confirming Mr. *Toland*'s notion; speaking of the admirable temperature of the air there, not subject to such extremities, such sudden changes, as even in *Britain* itself. There are such temples as ours there.

*Arnobius* in VI. speaking of the origin of temples, "We don't, says he, make temples to the Gods, as is we design'd to shelter them from the rain, the wind, the sun: but that we may therein present ourselves before them, and by our prayers, after a sort, speak to them as if present." We may well affirm this of our temple, built after the manner of the patriarchal ones, tho' probably an improvement, and somewhat more magnificent. Ours consists of two ovals and two circles. Many in our island, which I suppose older than *Stonehenge*, consist of one oval, or niche-like figure made of three stones only, (of which our *adytum* is a more magnificent specimen) and a circle of rude stones fix'd in the ground; of which our work, crown'd with a circular cornish, is a more magnificent specimen. Sometime I meet with a niche without a circle, sometime a circle without a niche. We may well say, the circle is analogous to our chapels, churches, or cathedrals, according to their different magnitude; the niches correspond to our choirs, altars, and more sacred part of the sacred building, the more immediate place of the residence of the Deity. They are what now the *Turks* and *Arabians* call the *kebla*, deriv'd, as we said before, from the patriarchal practice, and particularly from the great patriarch *Abraham*. I doubt not but the altars which he and his posterity made, mention'd in scripture, were a stone upon the ground before three set in a niche-like figure, and the whole inclos'd in a circle of stones. At other times they set only one stone for a *kebla*, as sometime our ancestors did likewise. This practice was propagated generally among all ancient nations. Among many it was forgotten, or not practised, where they had but little religion at all. Among others, after idolatry had prevail'd with them, they thought all former manners of worship like their own, and mistook the stones which were *kebla*'s or places of worship, for the objects of worship. Hence *Maximus* of *Tyre* says, the *Arabians* worshipp'd he knew not what, for he saw only a great stone. Which, no doubt, was the *kebla* toward which they directed their devotion, as they had learnt from *Abraham*, or the like patriarchal ancestors. So *Pausanias* in *Achaicis* says, the ancient *Greeks* worshipp'd unhewn stones instead of statues; more particularly among the *Pharii*, near the statue of *Mercury*, were 30 square stones, which they worshipp'd. If our author could not make his narration agreeable to common sense, he might well mistake this ancient patriarchal temple, somewhat like ours of *Stonehenge*, for a circle of deities: he himself being a stranger to any other than image-worship. I shall handle this matter more largely hereafter, and now let us descend again from the temple to the *cursus*. Only I would close this chapter with this short reflection. This avenue is proof enough (is there needed any) that our work is a temple, not a monument, as some writers would have it. But it requires no formal confutation.

Plate 21. An inward View of Stonehenge or Side view of the cell. AA the altar.

# CHAP. IX.

*Of the* Cursus. *Games exercis'd on holy festivals. The Druids understood geometry.*

ABOUT half a mile north of *Stonehenge*, across the first valley, is the *cursus* or *hippodrom*, which I discover'd august 6. 1723. 'Tis a noble monument of antiquity: and illustrates very much the preceding account of *Stonehenge*. It was the universal custom, to celebrate games, feasts, exercises and sports, at their more publick and solemn meetings to sacrifice. Which was done quarterly and anniversarily, at certain stated seasons of the year. *Macrob. Satur.* I. says, "Upon holy days dedicated to the gods, there are sacrifices, feasts, games and festivals. For a sacred solemnity is, when sacrifices are offer'd to the gods, or holy feastings celebrated, or games perform'd to their honour, or when holy days are observ'd." This great work is included between two ditches running east and west in a parallel, which are 350 foot asunder. When I mention 350 foot, I speak in the gross, and as we should set it down in an *English* scale: but if we look into where I have given a comparative view of our *English* foot, and the most ancient cubit; at first sight we discern, this measure means 200 of the Druid cubits. This *cursus* is a little above 10000 foot long: that is, it is made of 6000 Druid cubits in length. A most noble work, contriv'd to reach from the highest ground of two hills, extended the intermediate distance over a gentle valley: so that the whole cursus lies conveniently under the eye of the most numerous quantity of spectators. To render this more convenient for sight, it is projected on the side of rising ground, chiefly looking southward toward *Stonehenge*. A delightful prospect from the temple, when this vast plain was crouded with chariots, horsemen and foot, attending these solemnities, with innumerable multitudes! This *cursus*, which is two miles long, has two entrances (as it were:) gaps being left in the two little ditches. And these gaps, which are opposite to each other, in the two ditches, are opposite to the strait part of *Stonehenge* avenue.

I mention'd before, that at the bottom of the strait part of *Stonehenge* avenue in the valley, the avenue divides itself into two parts. One goes directly east toward *Radfin*, the other goes northwestward, and enters our *cursus* nearly at the same distance west from the gaps or entrances before-mention'd: as those gaps are from the east end of the *hippodrom*. These gaps being at a convenient distance from that east end, may be thought to be in the nature of distance posts. It seems to me, that the turf of the adjacent ground on both sides, has been originally taken off, and laid on the whole length of this *cursus*, because it appears somewhat higher in level. Tho' this was an incredible labour, yet a fine deign for the purpose of running. The earth of the *vallum* is likewise thrown inward.

The eat' end of the *cursus* is compos'd of a huge body of earth, a bank or long barrow, thrown up nearly the whole breadth of the *cursus*. This seems to be the plain of session, for the judges of the prizes, and chief of the spectators. The west end of the *cursus* is curv'd into an arch, like the end of the *Roman circus's*. And there probably the chariots ran round, in order to turn again. And there is an obscure barrow or two, round which they return'd, as it were, a *meta*.

This is the finest piece of ground that can be imagin'd for the purpose of a horse-race. The whole is commanded by the eye of a spectator in any part. In the middle is a valley, and pretty steep at present: yet only so, as that a *British* charioteer may have a good opportunity of showing that dexterity, spoken of by *Cæsar*. But the exquisite softness of the turf prevents any great damage by a fall. The ground of it hereabouts declines somewhat northward. The main part of this *hippodrom* is upon a gentle ridge running east and west. This render'd the place cooler.

On the southern ridge, toward the west end of it, are many considerable barrows: but none towards the east end, for that would obstruct the view of *Stonehenge*. There are many barrows but of no considerable bulk, on the north-side, upon the extensive ascent, toward the great north long barrow. This magnificent work of the *cursus* is drawn due east and west: except a small variation of 4 or 5 degrees southward from the east. If we measure along the bank from the eastern *meta*, at 700 cubits exactly, we come over against the middle line of the strait part of the avenue to *Stonehenge*: 500 cubits further conducts us to the gaps or opposite entrances, I before mention'd; which we suppose as distance posts. The whole interval between the eastern *meta* and these gaps, is 1200 cubits. At 1000 cubits more, we come to the place where the west wing of the avenue enters the southern ditch of the *cursus*. That west wing too, is just 1000 cubits long to its union, with the strait part of *Stonehenge* avenue. Likewise the strait part of *Stonehenge* avenue is just TAB. XXVIII. cubits long, as mention'd in its proper place. This west wing begins, in the bottom of that valley, which crosses the middle of the *cursus* and sweeping along by the bottom of the hill, in a gentle curve, meets with the lower end of the strait part of *Stonehenge* avenue, where the wing or avenue unites to it, with an equal angle. So that the whole work is laid out with great judgment and symmetry; and curiously adapted to the ground, which was well consider'd, before the plot was mark'd out, by the first surveyors. From the bottom of the valley crossing the middle of the *cursus*, to the western *meta* is 3800 cubits more, making in the whole 6000 cubits. The north end of the eastern *meta* does not extend so far as the northern bank of the *cursus*: I suppose, the reason is, that there might be liberty that way, to stop the horses, at the end of the course. Therefore they set out, on the south side of the *cursus* and return'd by the north side. I observe the ditch and bank towards the eastern end of the *cursus* much obscur'd, by the trampling of men and horses, frequenting the spectators here: this being the most throng'd.

The *Cursus* is directly north from *Stonehenge*: so exactly, that the meridian line of *Stonehenge* passes precisely thro' the middle of the *Cursus*. And when we stand in the grand entrance of *Stonehenge* and observe the two extremities of the *Cursus* the eastern and western *meta*, they are each exactly 60 degrees from the meridian line; on each hand: making a third part of the circle of the horizon. By which we see, the Druids well understood the geometry of a circle, and its measure of 360 parts.

*Pausanias* in *Beotic.* says, 'among the Thebans, by the gate *Prætis* is the *Gymnasium* of *Jolaus* and likewise the stadium, which is a bank of earth thrown up, such as that at *Olympia* and of the *Laurii*. In the same place is the heroical monument of *Jolaus*. A little beyond, to the right is the *hippodrom*, and in it *Pindar's* monument. The same author in *Arcad.* VIII. writes, that before the walls of *Mantinea*, in a field, was a stadium made for horse-races, in honour of *Antinous*. Not far from it was the temple of *Neptunus equestris* and others.' So that we see it was the manner of the ancient *Greeks* thus to define their places for sports by banks of earth, and that near their temples.

After the *Romans* had borrow'd the use of the *British* chariots for travelling and the like, they us'd them too in the *Circensian* games. Thus *Sidonius Apollinaris* his poem upon it, *Lib.* XXII.

*Instant verberibus simul regentes,*
*Jamque & pectora prona de covinno*
*Extensi rapiuntur.*----------------------

Plate 22: An inward view of the Cell obliquely

Again,

*Tunc cœtus juvenum sed aulicorum*
*Elœi simulachra torva Carapi*
*Exercent, spatiantibus quadrigis.*
*------tandem murmura buccinæ strepentis*
*Suspensas tubicen vocans quadrigis,*
*Effundit celeres in arva currus.*
*Hinc agger sonat, hinc Arar resultat,*
*Hinc se se pedes atque eques reflectit,*
*Stridentum & moderator essedorum.*

Such, we may well imagine, was the scene of this place, in ancient days. And as the poet mentions the river *Arar*, I may take notice, in passing, that I have seen, several other places of sports and racings, which I take to have belong'd to the ancient *Britons*. As particularly those two great banks call'd *Rawdikes* in the meadow near *Leicester*, which spectators look

111

on as unaccountable. Another such work, I have seen in the meadow by *Dorchester*, the ancient *Roman* city and episcopal see, in *Oxfordshire*. Both are by the side of rivers. Another upon the river *Lowther* by *Perith* in *Cumberland*.

These places by rivers, were more agreeable to the *Greek* taste, as in a hotter country. Another like place of sports, was in the chalky valley just without the town of *Royston*, on the south side of it, by the *London* road. The old *Roman* road there, or *Hermen-street* passes over one corner of the work, as being of later date. I may, perhaps, describe these more largely, another time. We read in *Homer* and *Virgil* that races were celebrated at funerals.

# CHAP. X.

*Of the barrows, or sepulchral* tumuli *about* Stonehenge. *Generally set in groups, which are family burial places; and in sight of* Stonehenge. *They are single burial places. How the body is posited. What has been found in digging into these barrows.*

I COME in the last place to speak of the barrows, observable in great numbers, round *Stonehenge*. We may very readily count fifty at a time, in sight, from the place; easily distinguishable: but especially in the evening, when the sloping rays of the sun shine on the ground beyond them. These barrows are the artificial ornaments of this vast and open plain. And it is no small entertainment for a curious person, to remark their beauties, their variety in form and magnitude, their situation. They are generally of a very elegant *campaniform* shape, and done with great nicety. There is likewise a great variety in their shape, and turn, and in their diameters, in their manner of composition. In general, they are always upon elevated ground, and in sight of the temple of *Stonehenge*. For they all regard it. This shews, *they* are but superficial inspectors of things, that fancy from hence, great battels on the plain; and that these are the tumultuary burials of the slain. Quite otherwise; they are assuredly, the single sepulchres of kings, and great personages, buried during a considerable space of time, and that in peace. There are many groups of them together, and as family burial places; the variety in them, seems to indicate some note of difference in the persons there interr'd, well known in those ages. Probably the priests and laity were someway distinguish'd; as well as different orders and stations in them. Most of the barrows have little ditches around, extremely well defin'd. In many is a circular ditch 60 cubits in diameter, with a very small *tumulus* in the center. 60 or even too cubits is a very common

113

diameter in the large barrows. Often, they are set in rows, and equidistant, so as to produce a regular and pretty appearance, and with some particular regard to the parts of the temple, the avenues, or the *cursus*. For instance, where the avenue begins at the first elevation, from *Radfin* ford, advancing towards *Stonehenge*, seven large and flat old barrows are on the right hand of the avenue, towards the east end of the *cursus*, seven large barrows TAB XXIV. of a newer shape, are on the left hand: both these groups before spoken of, are plac'd in a similar manner, in regard to the avenue, and as wings or openings to it. Upon every range of hills, quite round *Stonehenge*, are successive TAB. XXXIII. groups of barrows, for some miles: and we may even observe, that great barrow by Lord *Pembroke's* park at *Wilton*, which I call the tomb of *Carvilius*, is set within view of *Stonehenge*.

In 1722, my late Lord *Pembroke*, Earl *Thomas*, who was pleas'd to favour my inquiries at this place, open'd a barrow, in order to find the position of the body observ'd in these early days. He pitch'd upon one of those south of *Stonehenge*, close upon the road thither from *Wilton:* and on the east side of the road. 'Tis one of the double barrows, or where two are inclos'd in one ditch: one of those, which I suppose the later kind, and of a fine turn'd bell-fashion. On the west side, he made a section from the top to the bottom, an intire segment, from center to circumference. The manner of composition of the barrow was good earth, quite thro', except a coat of chalk of about two foot thickness, covering it quite over, under the turf. Hence it appears, that the method of making these barrows was to dig up the turf for a great space round, till the barrow was brought to its intended bulk. Then with the chalk, dug out of the environing ditch, they powder'd it all over. So that for a considerable time, these barrows must have look'd white: even for some number of years. And the notion of sanctity annex'd to them, forbid people trampling on them, till perfectly settled and turf'd over. Hence the neatness of their form to this day. At the top or center of this barrow, not above three foot under the surface, my Lord found the skeleton of the interr'd; perfect, of a reasonable size, the head lying toward *Stonehenge*, or northward.

The year following, in order to prosecute this inquiry, by my Lord's order, I begun upon a barrow north of *Stonehenge*, in that group south of the *cursus*. 'Tis one of the double barrows there: and the more easterly, and lower of the two: likewise somewhat less. It was reasonable to believe, this was the sepulture of a man and his wise: and that the lesser was the female: and so it prov'd, at least a daughter. We made a large cut on the top from east to west. After the turf taken off, we came to the layer of chalk, as before, then fine garden mould. About three foot below the surface, a layer of flints, humouring the convexity of the barrow. These flints are gather'd from the surface of the downs in some places, especially where it has been plow'd. This being about a foot thick, rested on a layer of soft mould another foot: in which was inclos'd an urn full of bones. This urn was of unbak'd clay, of a dark reddish colour: crumbled into pieces. It had been rudely wrought with small mouldings round the verge, and other circular channels on the outside, with several indentures between, made with a pointed tool, as depicted where I have drawn all the sorts of things found in this barrow. The bones had been burnt, and crouded all together in a little heap, not so much as a hat crown would contain. The collar bone, and one side of the under-jaw are grav'd in their true magnitude. It appears to have been a girl of about 14 years old, by their bulk and the great quantity of female ornaments mix'd with the bones, all which we gather'd.

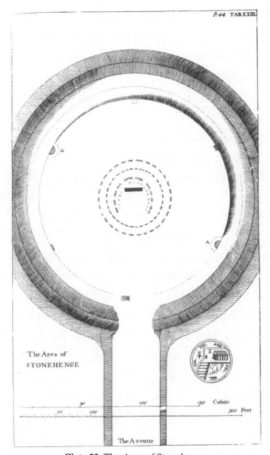

Plate 23. The Area of Stonehenge

Beads of all sorts, and in great number, of glass of divers colours, most yellow, one black. Many single, many in long pieces notch'd between, so as to resemble a string of beads, and these were generally of a blue colour. There were many of amber, of all shapes and sizes, flat squares, long squares, round, oblong, little and great. Likewise many of earth, of different shapes, magnitude and colour, some little and white, many large and flattish like a button, others like a pully. But all had holes to run a string thro', either thro' their diameter, or sides. Many of the button sort seem to have been cover'd with metal, there being a rim work'd in them, wherein to turn the edge of the covering. One of these was cover'd with a thin film of pure gold. These were the young lady's ornaments. And had all undergone the fire: so that what would easily consume fell to pieces as soon as handled. Much of the amber burnt half thro'. This person was a heroin, for we found the head of her javelin in brass. At bottom are two holes for the pins that fastned it to the staff. Besides, there was a sharp bodkin, round at one end, square at the other, where it went into a handle. I still preserve whatever is permanent of these trinkets. But we recompos'd the ashes of the illustrious defunct, and cover'd them with earth. Leaving visible marks at top, of the barrow having been open'd, to dissuade any other from again disturbing them: and this was our practice in all the rest.

Then we op'd the next barrow to it, inclos'd in the same ditch, which we suppos'd the husband or father of this lady. At fourteen inches deep, the mould being mix'd with chalk, we came to the intire skeleton of a man. The skull and all the bones exceedingly rotten and perish'd, thro' length of time. Tho' this was a barrow of the latest sort, as we conjecture. The body lay north and south, the head to the north, as that Lord *Pembroke* open'd.

Next, I went westward, to a group of barrows whence *Stonehenge* bears east north-east. Here is a large barrow ditch'd about, but of an ancient make. On that side next *Stonehenge* are ten lesser, small, and as it were crouded together. South of the great one is another barrow, larger than those of the group, but not equalling the first. It would seem, that a man and his wife were bury'd in the two larger, and that the rest were of their children or dependants. One of the small ones, 20 cubits in diameter, I cut thro', with a pit nine foot in diameter, to the surface of the natural chalk, in the center of the barrow; where was a little hole cut. A child's body (as it seems) had been burnt here, and cover'd up in that hole: but thro' the length of time consum'd. From three foot deep, we found much wood ashes soft and black as ink, same little bits of an urn, and black and red earth very rotten. Some small lumps of earth red as vermilion: some flints burnt thro'. Toward the bottom a great quantity of ashes and burnt bones. From this place I could count 128 barrows in sight.

Going from hence more southerly, there is a circular dish-like cavity dug in the chalk, 60 cubits in diameter, like a barrow revers'd. 'Tis near a great barrow, the least of the south-western group. 'Tis between it, and what I call the bushbarrow, set with thorn-trees. This cavity is seven feet deep in the middle, extremely well turn'd, and out of it, no doubt, the adjacent barrow is dug. The use of it seems to have been a place for sacrificing and feasting in memory of the dead, as was the ancient custom. 'Tis all overgrown with that pretty shrub *erica vulgaris*, now in flower, and smelling like honey. We made a large cross section in its center upon the cardinal points; we found nothing but a bit of red earthen pot.

We dug up one of those I call Druid's barrows, a small tump inclos'd in a large circular ditch. I chose that next to bushbarrow, westward of it. *Stonehenge* bears hence north-east. We made a cross section ten foot each way, three foot broad over its center, upon the cardinal points. At length we found a squarish hole cut into the solid chalk, in the center of the *tumulus*. It was three foot and a half, *i.e.* two cubits long, and near two foot broad, *i.e.* one cubit: pointing to *Stonehenge* directly. It was a cubit and half deep from the surface. This was the *domus exilis Plutonia* cover'd with artificial earth, not above a foot thick from the surface. In this little grave we found all the burnt bones of a man, but no signs of an urn. The bank of the circular ditch is on the outside, and is 12 cubits broad. The ditch is 6 cubits broad (the Druid's staff) the area is 70 cubits in diameter. The whole 100.

I open'd another of these of like dimensions, next to that Lord *Pembroke* first open'd, south of *Stonehenge*. We found a burnt body in a hole in the chalk, as before. Mr. *Roger Gale* was with me.

In some other barrows I open'd, were found large burnt bones of horses and dogs, along with human. Also of other animals as seem'd; of fowl, hares, boars, deer, goats, or the like. And in a great and very flat old fashion'd barrow, west from *Stonehenge*, among such matters, I found bits of red and blue marble, chippings of the stones of the temple. So that probably the interr'd was one of the builders. *Homer* tells us of *Achilles* slaying horses and dogs, at the funeral of his friend *Patroclus*.

Lord *Pembroke* told me of a brass sword dug up in a barrow here, which was sent to *Oxford*. In that very old barrow near little *Ambersbury*, was found a very large brass weapon of 20 pounds weight, like a pole-ax. Said to be given to col. *Wyndham*. In the great long barrow farthest north from *Stonehenge*, which I call north long barrow, and supposd to be an Arch-druid's, was found one of those brass instruments call'd *celts*, which I hold to belong to the Druids, wherewith they cut off the misletoe, as before mention'd. Mr. *Stallard* of *Ambersbury* gave it to Lord *Burlington*, now in Sir *Hans Sloane*'s cabinet: 13 inches long. They dug a cell in a barrow east of *Ambersbury*, and it was inhabited for some time. There they found all the bones of a horse. This is the sum of what is most material, that fell within my observation, relating to the barrows about *Stonehenge*. We find evidently, these ancient nations had the custom of burning their dead bodies, probably before the name of *Rome*. So lachrymatories we read of in scripture, ancienter than *Greek* or *Roman* times, *Psalm* lvi.

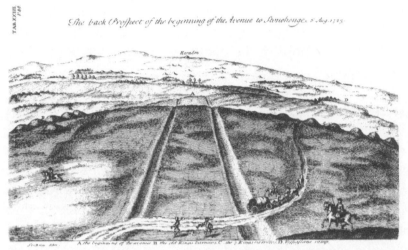

Plate 24. The back Prospect of the beginning of the Avenue to Stonehenge, 6 Aug. 1723. A. the beginning of the avenue. B. the old Kings barrows. C. the 7 Kings barrows. D. Vespasians camp.

# CHAP. XI.

*Of the original name of* Stonehenge, *and a conjecture of the general time of building such kind of works. Of* Wansdike, *by whom made and when. Of* Vespasian's *camp.* Stonehenge *was call'd the* Ambers, *or Main* Ambres: *which mean the anointed stones, i.e. the consecrated, the sacred stones? The meaning of the word* Ambrosia. *The* Tyrian Hercules *brought the* Druids *hither, with* Abraham's *religion.* Apher *a grandson of* Abraham's, *his companion.*

I Have inform'd the reader, to the best of my skill, what was, and what is the state of *Stonehenge*, both above, and below ground. I apprehend, it will be expected, that I should say somewhat, concerning the antiquity and time of erecting these works, especially of *Stonehenge*. But what can we say, of a matter so very remote? where the oldest memoirs and reports of the oldest nation inhabiting the island, can give us no satisfaction about it: but are as far to seek, as to the founders of this wonderful work, as we are, at this time, and are forced to apply to magic: in order to account for it. Notwithstanding, I shall endeavour to satisfy the readers curiosity, in this point, as well as I can; by giving him my own opinion about it. Not doubting of his candour, in so arduous an attempt: which may perhaps be an amusement to him, whether it gains his belief, or not. Therefore, I shall recite, in short, what occurs to me, on this subject. 1. As to the antiquity of these temples in general. 2. Of the time of founding *Stonehenge*.

The former will anticipate, in some sort, what I promis'd, in treating of the temples of the Druids in general. But I am naturally led to it, here, by observing, that the name of the adjacent town of *Ambersbury*, points out a relation to the work of *Stonehenge*, and to the ancient name of it. For as we took notice at first, the present name of *Stonehenge*, is purely *Saxon*, given by our latest ancestors, by a people wholly strangers to the purport of the thing, that had no notion, no report of its having once been a sacred place; and signifies no more than hanging-stones, or a stone-gallows. The ancient *Britons* call'd it *choir-gaur*, which the *Monks* latiniz'd into *chorea gigantum*, the giants dance; a name suited to the marvelous notion they had of the structure, or of the reports of magic, concern'd in raising it. But I had rather chuse to think *choir gaur* in *Welsh*, truly means, the great church; the cathedral, in our way of speaking. A general title, which the *Welsh* inhabitants, the remnants of the *Belgæ*, conquer'd by the *Romans*, gave it; as well knowing the true use of it, and even frequenting it in a religious way. Tho' they had driven off the first possessors of it, and the builders: I mean in *Divitiacus* his time, or sooner, before the *Roman* invasion.

There is a very plain reason: that *Stonehenge* was built, before the *Wansdike* was made, and *that* was the last boundary of the *Belgic* kingdom in *Britain*. The stones of which *Stonehenge* is compos'd, were fetcht from beyond that boundary, consequently *then* an enemies country. It seems not improbable, that the *Wansdike* was made, when this *Belgic* kingdom was at its height, and that time we may well guess at, from *Cæsar*. "He tells us in *Bell. Gall. Lib.* II. 4. the *Belgæ* are of *German* original. By force of arms, they possess'd themselves of the countries, south of the *Rhine* and towards the ocean, driving out the *Gauls*. They were a very warlike nation, and could produce 100,000 men in arms. That one of their kings *Divitiacus*, in the memory of some then living, obtain'd the government, both of great part of Gaul and in Britain too." I believe the *Belgæ* and *Sicambri*, all one people of *German* original. Our *Welsh* call themselves *Cymri*, and from them *Cumberland* has its name. It is very just to think this *Wansdike* was made in the time of *Divitiacus*, both because of the greatness of the work, suiting so potent a prince, and because it is the laic boundary: after that time, the *Roman* power swallowing up all divisions.

I judge, we may reasonably place the time of making the *Wansdike*, about 50 years before *Cæsar* wrote, we may say AUC. 650. *Divitiacus* probably ordered it to be made in person. And it seems to have been drawn from the upper end of the *Tees* river, about *Whit-church*, and *Andover*, in *Hampshire:* to the *Avon* river, about *Bristol*. These two rivers and the *Wansdike* separated the *Belgic* kingdom from the old *Celtic Britons*. They by this means, were driven from this beautiful country, and from their stately temple of *Stonehenge*, by these powerful invaders. It is remarkable enough, that the inhabitants of *Somersetshire*, the ancient seat of the *Belgæ*, retain still the *Belgic*, liquidating pronunciation, *v* consonant for *f. z* for *s.*

The *Devizes* is a town in the middle of the length of *Wansdike*, very probably erected, among others, to secure this ditch or fortification. It seems to have been the capital fort or frontier town, and to have its name from the king, as a trophy or monument of his power: built by him in person. *Anonymus Ravennas* may possibly call it *Punctuobice*, but we have no certainty, that his copy retains the word uncorrupt, or that he transcribed it right: nor what alteration the *Romans* made in the original word, nor what was made in the later and barbarous times. However there seems enough therein, as well as in the present name of the town, to countenance our conjecture. The former part of the word *punctuo*, which Mr. *Baxter* thinks monstrous, may come, perhaps, from the *German* word *pooghen*, which signifies an arduous work, and might regard the castle here, which is said to have been once, the strongest in *Europe*. *Neubringensis* calls it *Divisæ*.

They tell us legendary forces of its being built by an old *British* king.

*Divisus* was probably the name of this *Belgic* Monarch, or *Duiguis:* as *Gluiguis* king of *Demetia* in *Wales* is wrote *Glivisus* in *Toland*, p. 186. and the termination may have been form'd into *Latin*, from the *Celtic* word *taeog dux*. Whence, perhaps, the *Etruscan Tages*, so much boasted of in their antiquities; likewise the modern *Doge* of *Venice*. So that *Divitiacus* may well be *Divisus dux*. The name of the *Wansdike*, I shewed to be purely *Celtic*.

It is an ancient oriental custom to make these boundary ditches. Thus the land belonging to the several tribes of *Israel* was marked out by a ditch, as we read in the accounts of the holy land. Particularly the author of *le voyage de la terre sainte*, printed 1675. Paris, p. 57. says, "he travell'd five or six miles along such a ditch going from *Joppa* to *Jerusalem*, which parted the tribes of *Benjamin* and *Judah*." 'Tis recited *Joshua* XV.

The monkish writers make much ado about *Aurelius Ambrosius*, a christian king of the *Britons* (in the time of our great ancestor *Hengist*) building *Stonehenge*, by the help of *Merlin Ambrosius* the magician, in memory of the *British* nobility slain treacherously by *Hengist*, at *Ambresbury*. Some say the fact was committed *ad pagum Ambri*, others call it *cœnobium Ambrij*, others *ad montem Ambrij*. One while they refer the name to *Ambrosius*, another time to an Abbot *Ambrius*, and this was among our *Roman British* ancestors, who were christians. They add too, that *Merlin* fetch'd these stones out of *Ireland*, that they had been brought before, out of *Africa* into *Ireland:* that he set them up here in the same form, by art magic; and that the stones were of a medicinal Virtue. These matters we read in *Girald. Cambrens*. de admirand. Hib. c. 18.

*Higden's* Polychron. v. *Geoff. Monmouth* VIII. *Matt .Westminster,* &c.

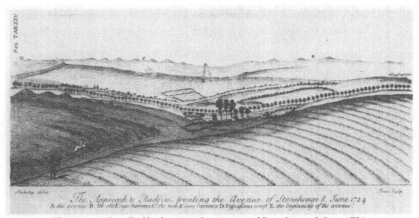

The Approach to Radfin fronting the Avenue of Stonehenge 8. June 1724.
A. the avenue. B. the old Kings barrows. C. The new Kings barrows. D. Vespasians camp. E. the
beginning of the avenue.

This calls to my memory, what the above-mention'd Dr. *Harwood* inform'd me, he had heard the great Sir *Christopher Wren* say, that there were such structures as *Stonehenge,* in *Africa,* being temples dedicate to *Saturn.* But I need not be tedious in observing, how absurd the *Monkish* reports are; of a christian king erecting *Stonehenge,* as a sepulchral monument for the *British* nobility, massacred in the monastery of *Ambresbury.* At the same time they say, their bodies were buried in the church-yard of the monastery. Nor how they confound the names of *Ambrosius* the king, *Ambrius* the abbot, the town, abby and mountain of *Ambry,* and perhaps of *Merlin* too, for one of them was call'd *Ambrosius.* But their affirming, the edifice came out of *Africa* into *Spain,* thence into *Ireland,* thence into *Britain,* and of its being erected here in the same form, by art magic; and that the stones are of a medicinal virtue: these notions lead us to the original truth, of the Druid founders, and that *Stonehenge* had originally, the name of *Ambres,* and from it the adjacent town of *Ambresbury* had its name.

To pursue this matter a little further. Between *Stonehenge* and the town, hanging over the river, upon elevated ground is a fine and ancient camp, commonly call'd *Vespasian's,* and not without much probability, attributed to him. We have often had occasion to mention it before. That great man, destin'd by providence for executing his final vengeance, on the people of the *Jews,* and thereby accomplishing our Saviour's predictions; by his successes in this place, pav'd a road to the imperial dignity. Having conquer'd the isle of *Wight,* he pursued his good fortune, higher up into this country, where he made this camp, and another across the heath, call'd *Yanesbury;* which seems to retain the latter part of his name. The camp we are speaking of near *Ambresbury,* is an oblong square, nicely placed upon a flexure of the river, which closes one side and one end of it. There is an old barrow inclos'd in it, which, doubtless was one of those belonging to this plain, and to the temple of *Stonehenge,* before this camp was made. It is pretty to observe, that the road from *Stonehenge* to *Ambresbury,* runs upon the true *via prætoria* of the camp. The Generals tent or *prætorium* was in that part south of the road, between it and the river, toward little *Ambresbury.* There is another gate of the camp, at the lower end, northward, the *porta prætoria ordinaria,* in the Roman language. Now I apprehend, that *Stonehenge* was originally call'd the *Ambres,* from thence this camp was call'd *Ambresburgh,* and thence the name of the town underneath.

Mr. *Camden* writes, "that near *Pensans* in *Cornwall,* is a very remarkable stone, call'd *main Ambre,* which tho' it be of a vast bigness, yet you may move it with one finger: notwithstanding a great number of men cannot remove it from its place. The name is interpreted the stone of *Ambrosius.*" A picture of it in *Norden*'s history of *Cornwall*, p. 48. I have seen one of these rocking stones, as call'd commonly, in *Derbyshire*. Mr. *Toland* in his history of the *Druids*, mentions it too, and says there are such in *Wales* and in *Ireland*, Sir *Robert Sibbald* mentions them in *Scotland*, all rightly judg'd to have been done by the Druids. Sir *Robert* speaking of the rocking stone near *Balvaird* (or the *Bards* town) in *Fife*: "I am inform'd (says he) that this stone was broken by the usurper *Cromwell*'s soldiers. And it was discover'd then, that its motion was perform'd, by a yolk extuberant in the middle of the under surface of the uppermost stone which was inserted in a cavity, in the surface of the lower stone." This is the artifice of the stones at *Stonehenge*, but applied here by the Druids for a moveable principle, as there, for stability. I call them mortaise and tenon: and before observ'd them to be of an egg-like form; which Sir *Robert* calls a yolk. The *Main Amber* in *Cornwall* was likewise destroy'd in the civil wars, by one of *Oliver*'s governors. These reformers had a notion of these works being superstitious matters. *Main Ambre* is *lapis Ambrosius*, or *petra Ambrosia*. And that name leads us to consider the famous *petræ Amhrosiæ*, on the coins of the city of *Tyre*. A specimen of them, I have drawn on the *Plate* following.

These, and many more of the like sort, struck by the city of *Tyre*, in honour of their founder *Hercules*, may be seen in *Vaillant*'s second Volume of colony coins, *pag.* 69, 148, 218, 251, 337.

They represent two great, rough stones, call'd *petræ ambrosiæ*, with an altar before them, and an olive tree; *Hercules* the hero of *Tyre*, the famous Navigator of antiquity, their founder, sacrificing. On some of the coins *petræ ambrosiæ* wrote in Greek. He is represented indeed like the *Greek Hercules*, but in the latter times of the *Roman* empire, when these coins were struck, they at *Tyre* were as far to seek about the true meaning and origin of their first antiquities, as we of ours. And what knowledge they had of them, was from legendary reports of the *Greeks*, who chiefly, among the heathens, had the knack of writing. These reports, as we may find in *Nonnus* his *Dionysiacs*, 40. and 41. acquaint us, that *Hercules* invented shipping, as a latin poet too intimates, *Tibullus*.

*Prima ratem ventis credere docta Tyrus.*

They acquaint us that he ordered *Tyre* to be built, where the *petræ ambrosiæ* stood, which were two moveable rocks, standing by an olive tree. He was to sacrifice on them, and they should become fixt and stable: rather, the City should be built with happy auspice, and become permanent.

Here are our *Main Ambres*, made artfully moveable, a kind of altars, or pillars, the same as the pillars of *Hercules* so fam'd, and as little understood. They were the original patriarchal altars, for libations and sacrifices, and mean, in general, their Altars, whether moveable or immoveable: or as we may speak, their temples, which imply an altar properly, inclosed with stones and a ditch, or ground dedicated and set apart for public celebration of religious rites. For the word *Ambrosius* means in general, consecrated, dedicated to religious use.

Beside the *petræ ambrosiæ* of *Tyre,* and our *main ambres* of *Britain* and *Ireland,* we meet with another in *Hephæstion's* History III. 3. "Speaking of *Hercules,* he mentions the *Gygonian* stone, as he calls it, near the ocean, which may be mov'd with the stalk of an *asphodel,* but can't be remov'd by any force." It seems this word *Gygonius* is purely *Celtic.* For *gwingog* signifies *motitans,* the rocking stone; and *gwgon* is what the boys with us call a gig, or little top. For these *Gygonian* stones are of that shape, pyramidal.

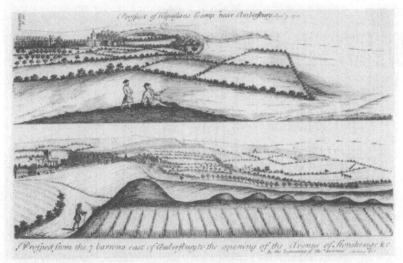

Plate 26. (above) Prospect of Vespasians Camp near Ambersbury. Aug. 7 1723
(below) Prospect from the 7 barrows east of Ambersbury to the opening of the Avenue of Stonehenge, &c. A. the beginning of the avenue.

No wonder these matters are well nigh lost, in the mist of extreme antiquity, when even the meaning of the word *ambrosius* was hardly known, either to the antients or moderns, till Mr. *Baxter* discover'd it, in his glossary. It signifies oil of roses, *rosaceum:* the most antient kind of perfume. In the 4th *Odyssy,* v. 445. *Edothea* a sea goddess, teaches *Menelaus* and his companions, to cure the odious smell of the sea calves.

Ἀμβεροίλυ ὑπὸ ῥῖνα ἐκάςω ϑῆκε φέρεσα
Ἡδυμάλα πνείοσαν.————— ————————

She put *ambrosia* to their noses, sweetly smelling. Again, in his hymn to *Venus*, the graces washt the goddess, and anointed her with oil ambrosial: such as becomes the immortals.

—————————ᾗ χεῖσαν ἐλαίω
Ἀμβερότω, οἷα Θεὺς ἐπενλω̂νϑεν αἰὲν ἐόντας.

Lastly, in *Iliad*. XXIII. *Venus* anoints *Hector*'s body with ambrosial oil of roses,

————— ῥοδόεντι ᾗ χεῖεν ἐλαίω
Ἀμβερόσω —————— ————

Which is a tautology. For from length of time, they scarce knew the true meaning of the word in *Homer*'s age.

*Virgil* seems to understand but somewhat of the original meaning of the word, speaking of *Venus*; her hair was anointed with ointment perfum'd.

> *Ambrosiæq; comæ divinum vertice odorem*
> *Spiravere* ————————— —————————————— *Æneid.*

In *Pliny* Nat. Hist. XIII. 1. we find the *oleum rhodinum* most antient, common and simple. And this is the true *ambrosia*, which from its very antient use in sacred rites, had almost lost its meaning; and was us'd to signify, one while, the food of the gods, another time, immortality; again, whatever is divine, or appropriate to the gods. But simply, it signifies oil of roses, still from its first use, in sacred matters, it imports anointed, in a religious sense; consecrated, dedicated. Then *main ambres, ambres, petræ ambrosiæ*, signify the stones anointed with holy oil, consecrated; or in a general sense a temple, altar, or place of worship.

The truth is, it was a patriarchal custom to consecrate their altars, pillars, or in a general word temples, by anointing with oil, either simple or perfum'd. Rose oil being the oldest, engross'd the general name of the action; so that a stone anointed with oil of roses, is a *main amber*, or *lapis ambrosius*. The same is an altar, or stone dedicate to religious use. The plural number, *petræ ambrosiæ*, import a church or temple, in our way of speaking.

We have an illustrious instance of this practice in the holy Scriptures, and the earliest. *Gen.* xxviii. This is not commonly understood by writers. 'Tis the moving and memorable history of young *Jacob*, sent away from his father's house alone, to take a long journey to some unknown relations. He came to a place, call'd afterward *Bethel*, and sleeping with his head on a stone for a pillow, had a celestial vision; and a promise from God, of the highest importance to him and all mankind. Awaking, he thought the place had been holy ground, where, perhaps, his grandfather *Abraham* had before-time built an altar; an house of God, or gate of heaven, as he elegantly names it. "Therefore he rose up early in the morning, which was one circumstance (in patriarchal times) of the work he was going about, and took the stone that he had put for his pillow, and set it up for a pillar; and poured oil upon the top of it, and called the place *Beth-el, i.e.* the house of God. Then he vowed, that if God would please to prosper him in his journey, and bring him back into his own country, he would build a temple there, and consecrate to God the tythe of his substance, as was the manner in those times."

This is in reality a votive, patriarchal temple, altar or house of God, which he not only vows to build, but at the same time endows it. The stone which *Jacob* anointed, was not an altar properly, lying on the ground whereon to make a libation, but he set it up as a pillar. It was one of the upright stones, which the scripture calls pillars, as standing of itself; a part of the circle of stones, inclosing the altar. And by the act of anointing, *Jacob* consecrated it, as the manner then was, defined it for a sacred purpose, as an earnest of his will in good time to fulfil it. And this he did fulfil, *chap.* xxxv. building the celebrated temple of *Bethel*. Here *Jeroboam* set up one of his golden calves. At last it was destroy'd by *Vespasian*.

In Exod. xxiv. 4. "we have an instance of *Moses* rising up early in the morning and building an altar, and setting up 12 pillars around it." This was before the tabernacle was made, which introduced the custom of cover'd temples.

But so famous was that patriarchal temple of *Jacob's*, which he built at *Bethel*; that the heathen called all their temples of that sort, when they were perverted to idolatrous purposes, *Bæthylia, lapides Bætyli*, and the like. Which indeed is but another manner of expressing *lapis Ambrosius*, or our *Main Ambre*. And according to custom, the fabulous *Greeks* having lost the true history of its origin, affix'd many strange stories to it; as of *Saturn* devouring such a stone, wrapt up in a skin, instead of his Son *Jupiter*: which seems to be form'd from the memory of praying at these places, in the name of the mediatorial deity, as the patriarchs did. And *Sanchoniathon* tells us, the god *Ouranus* deviled *Bætylia*, or animated stones. He means our rocking stones, *gygonian* stones. I shall show in my discourse on that subject, that by *Ouranus*, he means righteous *Noah*, who, according to patriarchal usage, builded an altar unto *Jehovah, Gen.* viii. 20. meaning one of these patriarchal temples. In time, by the corruption of mankind, these places were desecrated to idolatrous purposes; and writers pervert the intent of them. So that God Almighty, raising up the Mosaic Dispensation, was oblig'd to interdict the very use and practice of these open temples, and introduce the cover'd one of the tabernacle; by way of opposition to heathenism, as well as with other important views.

We find now the meaning of anointed stones in antiquity, and the olive-tree set by the stones on the *Tyrian* coins. As the very learned Author of *Archæologia Græca* observes, on the affair of consecration, "they were more or less sumptuous and expensive, as other parts of divine worship, according to the ability of the worshippers." Young *Jacob* a traveller us'd plain oil, part of his *viaticum*, others us'd perfum'd oil, or *ambrosia*. That author cites us from *Athenæus*, the method of consecrating *Jupiter Ctestias*'s statue with a libation call'd *ambrosia*: and others by anointing with oil, prayers and libations, *Exodus* xxx. 22. We have the holy precious ointment made under the *Jewish* dispensation for the like purpose. And we use such, for inauguration of our kings, to this day.

The *Tyrian Hercules* who built *Tyre* and set up the *petræ Ambrosiæ* in those coins, (if I mistake not) liv'd as early as the time, of *Jacob*'s anointing the stone at *Bethel*. The great *Bochart*, who penetrated very deep into the *Phœnician* learning, looks upon it as a clear matter, that in *Joshua*'s time, the *Phœnicians* sent innumerable colonies, into the mediterranean coasts, and even to the ocean. In the preface to his admirable work *Canaan*, he says, "he has a great suspicion, that colonies went abroad this way, before that time. Particularly, he asserts, that *Hercules*, in *Eusebius* sirnamed Desanaus, who was famous in *Phœnicia* before the *Exodus*,

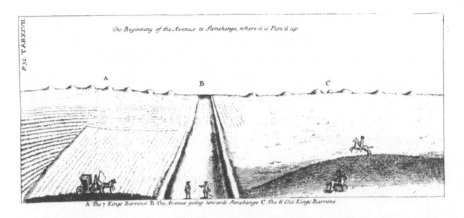

Plate 27. The Beginning of the Avenue to Stonehenge, where it is Plow'd up.
A. The 7 Kings Barrows. B. The Avenue going towards Stonehenge. C. The 6 Old Barrows.

is the same, who conquer'd *Antæus* in *Africa:* which in *Eusebius*, is set 56 years before. He is call'd *Hercules primus*, and that is 63 years before the *Exodus*, in *Eusebius*'s chronology." Again, he judges it to be 2000 years distance between the later *Roman* times and the first *Hercules*. Now from *Constantine* the great, 2000 years carries us up to *Jacob*'s time. And he proves, from *Aristotle de mirabilibus*, that *Hercules* built *Utica* in *Africa*, at that time; wherein *Eusebius* says he was famous in *Phœnicia*, and this must be when *Hercules* was old. He having conquer'd *Antæus* in that country, when he was young.

But I find in the same *Eusebius*, *Prometheus* is set 111 years still earlier, before the first mention of *Hercules*, this is during the life of the patriarch *Joseph*. *Prometheus* and *Atlas* were brothers, and students in Astronomy, with whom the story of *Hercules* is always conjoin'd. And so high at least, I must place the time of our *Tyrian Hercules*, who is the same as *Desanaus*. But *Marianus* transcribing *Eusebius* calls him *Dosenaus*. And *Hesychius* says *Dorsanes* is a name of *Hercules*, with the *Indians*. But by the *Indians*, it is likely, the *Phœnicians* and *Arabians* are meant; for the ancient *Greeks* call all the country to the east of the mediterranean sea, *India*. And then we may in some measure understand the report of *Ammianus Marcellinus*, who takes it from *Timagenes*, an old *Greek* Historian, but a *Syrian* by nation, speaking concerning the peopling of *Gaul*, "that the more ancient *Hercules* conducted the *Dorienses*, to the countries bordering on the ocean." Perhaps the *Dosareni* are meant, an *Arabian* nation, mention'd by *Ptolemy*. A Deity of the *Arabians* was called *Dusaris* or *Dosaris*, mention'd by *Step. Byzant, Suidas* and *Tertullian*. A difficult word, which *Bochart* cannot trace from the *Arabian* language; nor is it easy to say, what Deity he was. No wonder such matters are obscur'd, thro' so long distance of time. Some think him *Bacchus*, some *Mars*, and why not *Hercules?* for after mankind laps'd into idolatry, these three were much confounded.

I find sufficient testimony, of the *Tyrian Hercules* coming from *Arabia*, about the red sea, or having companions, that were natives of that country. For this reason they nam'd an island at the city of *Gadis*, which they built, *Erythia, Erythræa;* which *Pliny* IV. 22. says, was so called from the first possessors, the *Tyrians*, who came from the *Erythræan* sea: which is the red sea. *Solinus* says the same. That sea had its name from *Erythras*, as the *Greeks* and the same *Pliny* write; who is *Edom* or *Esau*, brother of *Jacob*. The words are synonymous, signifying red. The reports of *Hercules's* expedition to that island *Erythræa*, now *Cadiz*, is famous in all the old *Greek* writers.

This relation we have given of the *Tyrian Hercules*, that he lived about the time of *Abraham*, or soon after, according to *Eusebius's* chronology; that he came from about the red sea, and had companions in his travels, that lived thereabouts, is much confirm'd by what *Josephus* writes, from *Alexander Polyhistor;* who cites it from a very ancient author, called *Cleodemus*, sirnam'd *Malchus*, who wrote a history of the

*Jews*, agreeable with the *Mosaic*. He says, *Abraham* had several Sons by *Keturah*, he names *Apher*, *Suris* and *Japhra*. That *Apher* and *Japhra* were auxiliaries to *Hercules*, when he fought in *Lybia* against *Antæus*. That from *Apher* the country was nam'd *Africa*. That *Hercules* married his daughter, and begat of her *Dodorus*. *Josephus* in the same chap. of the first book of his antiquities, writes, that *Abraham* had six sons born of *Keturah*: men, heroic and wise. That they and their posterity were settled in *Troglodytis*, in the country of *Arabia fœlix*, reaching to the red sea. He makes *Opher* or *Apher* grandson to *Abraham*, by *Midian* his son. That *Apher* waged war in *Lybia* and conquer'd it, and plac'd his sons there, who call'd the Country *Africa* from their father, So *Schindler* in his lexicon, *pag.* 1361.

Making proper allowance for relations of such very antient matters, transmitted by historians of different countries, different languages, and so often transcribed and translated, before they come down to us; here is enough to confirm and explain, what we have before advanc'd: both as to time and place, and matter. And we cannot but see what relation our *Main Ambres* and the *gygonian* stone by the ocean, have to the *petræ ambrosiæ*, which *Hercules* set up at *Tyre:* which is the drift of my discourse. That very *gygonian* stone, for ought I see, may be our rocking-stone near *Pensans*, it stands by the sea-side. Nor do I see any absurdity, if we judge, that it was erected there, by *Hercules* in person. Near it is that other famous Druid temple call'd *Biscawoon*, consisting of 19 pillars in a circle and a central *kebla*. The entrance is made of 2 somewhat large stones, than the rest: not improbably one of the *Herculean* labours. It is affirm'd by the best authors, that our *Tyrian Hercules*, the more ancienter *Hercules*, built the city of *Gadis*, at *Cadiz* now. And where-ever *Hercules* came, there we read of his pillars. Thus *Avienus*.

*Hic Gadir urbs est, dicta Tartessus prius,*
*Hic sunt columnæ pertinacis Hercules.*

*Arrian* II. of the life of *Alexander*, remarks, "that *Gadis* was built by the *Phœnicians*. There was a temple of *Hercules*. The form, the sacrifices and ceremonies there perform'd, are all after the *Phœnician* manner." *Strabo* in his *Lib*. III. says there were two pillars in this temple, dedicate to *Hercules*; which the learned *Tristan* in his commentaries on medals, p. 384. says, he doubts not, but they were *petræ ambrosiæ*, in imitation of those of the same name, in the temple of *Hercules* of *Tyre*, which *Herodotus* in *Euterpe* speaks of. He appears to have been an extraordinary genius, and a man of great piety withal. Therefore where-ever he came, he made these patriarchal temples, or set up pillars of stone, as antiquity called them. Just as the patriarchal family did in the land of *Canaan*. And *Hercules* seems to me, to have been a great man, raised up by providence, to carry the reform'd patriarchal religion, to the extremest part of the then known western world. Here, I suppose, the religion of *Abraham* remain'd pure, for many ages, under the Druids, till perhaps corrupted by incursions from the continent. It is remarkable, that the *Romans*, who were so catholic, (different from those we now absurdly call *Roman* catholics) as to permit all religions, persecuted only that of the Druids, and the christian: whence we are naturally led to think, there was a good deal of resemblance. Indeed, the Druids are accused of human sacrifices. They crucified a man and burnt him on the altar; which seems to be a most extravagant act of superstition, deriv'd from some extraordinary notices they had of mankind's redemption: and perhaps from *Abraham*'s example misunderstood. But as to human sacrifices simply considered, the *Romans* themselves and all other nations upon earth at times, practis'd them.

To this *Hercules*, antiquity affixed very many names, from different notions of him, retain'd in different countries; and after idolatry took root, he was worshipp'd under those names of consecration, according to the old method. For instance, one of his names was *Palæmon*. *Palæmon*, says *Hesychius*, is *Hercules*. The *Greeks* made him a sea Deity, who had been so great a sea-captain. They call him *Melicerta*, which is his *Phœnician* name *Melcartus*, king of the city. *Ovid* tells us the story in *Met.* IV. *Nonnus* calls him *Afrochiton* starry-robed, from his being made a constellation in heaven. In the *Gallic* picture of him, which *Lucian* saw, he is represented with a sphere in one hand, under the name of *Ogmius*. Mr. *Toland* in his history of the Druids, shews us the true interpretation of that word, from the *Irish* language; after the learned had in vain attempted the explication of it. From thence we infer he brought the use of letters hither. *Cæsar* informs us, the Druids had them.

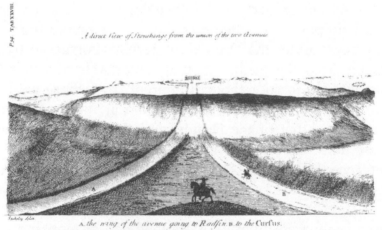

Plate 28. A direct View of Stonehenge from the union of the two Avenues.
A. the wing of the avenue going to Radfin. B. to the Cursus.

He is called *Assis*, by the easterns, which signifies the valiant: the same as *Hæsus* of the *Germans*.

Beside the patriarchal custom of building these places of worship, and consecrating them with oil, we find many other footsteps of that most ancient religion, in the history of *Hercules*. *Silius* speaking of the strange rites used in the *Gaditan* temple of *Hercules*, says, the priests officiated there barefooted, prais'd chastity, had no statues, us'd white linen surplices. And it is a notorious custom with the ancient *Phœnicians*, to pay tithe. Indeed they paid tythe to *Hercules*. Which only imports, that it was a precept and practice introduc'd by *Hercules*. And after they had deified *Hercules* they practis'd it toward him. This was a common method, when idolatry began. I shall treat more largely of these affairs; when I discourse expressly of the patriarchal religion. Likewise, I shall prove more fully, from chronological characters, that this *Hercules* liv'd at the time, we are speaking of, in the *canon Mosaicæ chronologiæ*. What I now recite, concerning these matters, I could not well avoid, as they in my apprehension. relate to the name of *Stonehenge*.

*Pliny Nat. Hist.* VII. 56. gives us a testimony, of our *Hercules*, under the name of *Melcartus*, (as *Bochart* rightly corrects it) first bringing tin into *Greece*, from the *Cassiterid* islands. By which the *British* are meant. The tin of *Tyre*, which the merchants of *Greece*, came to buy, at the fairs of that city, is mention'd *Ezekiel* xxvii. 12. which, no doubt, came from hence. But it is much earlier mention'd, among lead and other metals, when the *Midianites* had it in *Moses*'s time, *Numbers* xxxi. 22. the *Chaldee* and *Arabic* version there, use the word *kastira*, the *Hierosolymitan kistara*. No wonder the *Midianites* should then abound with tin: when we were told by *Josephus*, that *Apher* son of *Midian*, was one of *Hercules*'s companions. The LXX.in that passage of *Numbers* call it *κฉασίτεϱς*. But tin is mention'd earlier still, in *Job* xix. 24. and *Job* liv'd in this same country, on the borders of *Arabia*.

It is very evident from *Bochart*, that the *Phœnicians*, had sail'd quite round *Britain*, by what he writes of *Thule*. How then can we doubt but the great island, which they found in the extremest west, was *Britain?* but they kept their gainful navigation hither so secret, for many centuries, that even *Herodotus* the earliest *Greek* writer professes he knows not, whence the tin comes. *Britain* was the only country, where it could come from, in any quantity, as *Pliny* says. But from this great secrecy of the *Phœnicians*, we have lost the high antiquities of *Britain*, as unknown to the *Greeks*; the only heathen nation that had the address to commit things to writing. Therefore we must be content with what small remains of this kind, can be fish'd out of the wreck of time, by such conjectural methods, as antiquaries cannot avoid insisting on.

In *Devonshire* is *Hartland* point so call'd corruptly, as the excellent *Camden* observes, for *Herculis promontorium*. And upon the *Durham* sea coast is a town on a promontory call'd *Hartlepool*. A village call'd *Hart* near it. I take it to have been call'd by the *Greek* traders here *Heracleopolis*. And hence, probably came that fine old altar in *Greek*, dedicated to the *Tyrian Hercules*, which Mr. *Roger Gale* and I copied, in *Corbridge* church-yard.

From these and many other considerations of this kind, which I shall hereafter treat of more largely and professedly: I cannot but join in opinion with *Franc. Philelphus* in his epistles, and *Lilius Giraldus* in his *Hercules* mention'd by Mr. *Camden*, in the last quoted passage, and with many other writers, that the very ancient *Phœnician* or *Tyrian Hercules* conducted an eastern colony hither, upon the aborigines; with whom came the Druids, the builders of *Stonehenge* and the like works among us. And let this suffice for what I promis'd upon the first head of this chapter, *viz.* to speak of the antiquity of these works in general. 2. We are to speak of the time of founding *Stonehenge*.

# CHAP. XII.

*A conjecture about the time of the founding of* Stonehenge. *An uniform variation in setting these works, not to be accounted for, but by supposing the* Druids *us'd a magnetical compass. Their leader, the* Tyrian Hercules, *was possess'd of a compass-box. The oracle of* Jupiter Ammon *had a compass-box. The golden fleece at* Colchis *was a compass-box. Both these temples were founded by* Apher, Hercules *his companion, and grandson to* Abraham. Apher, Aphricus, *or* Phryxus *the same person, seems to have given name to* Britain. *The* Druids *set their temples and other works by it. The history of the mariner's compass, since that time. The history of the variation of the magnetic needle. A conjecture of the time of building* Stonehenge, *from thence.*

IN my Enquiries into these works of the antient *Druids* in our island, I observed a greater exactness in placing them, with regard to the quarters of the heavens, than one would expect, in works seemingly so rude; and in so remote an age, to which we must necessarily refer them. What more particularly mov'd my attention, was a certain variation from cardinal points, which I observed regular and uniform, in the works of one place. And that variation was different, in works of another place; yet equally regular and uniform in that place. Suppose (for instance) the works about *Abury* in *Wiltshire* generally vary 9 or 10 degrees to the left hand, from cardinal points: *i.e.* westward from the north. And the works at *Stonehenge* generally vary to the right hand, from cardinal points, and that to the quantity of 6 or 7 degrees. The principal diameter or groundline of *Stonehenge*, leading from the entrance, up the middle of the temple, to the high altar, (from which line the whole work is form'd) varies about that quantity southward of the north east point. The intent of the founders of *Stonehenge*, was to set the entrance full north east, being the point where the sun rises, or nearly, at the

summer solstice. As well because *that* is the farthest elonga-
tion of the great celestial luminary, northward; the comple-
ment of our earthly felicity, in ripening the fruits of the
earth: as because *then* they celebrated one of their principal
religious meetings or festivals, with sacrifices, publick
games, and the like. Such was the custom of all the antient
nations. The *Isthmian, Nemæan, Olympian, Pythian* games,
famous in the works of the learned nations: those of *Tyre* II.
*Maccabees* iv. 18. dedicated to their and our founder, the antient *Tyrian Hercules*, who, I suppose, conducted the first
*Phœnician* colony, with our *Druids*, into *Britain:* these were all
held at this time of the year. A custom continu'd from patriarchal times.

This exactness with which the *Druids* set their works, and
the uniformity of their variation, make me believe, this
variation was not the effect of chance or negligence.

By a superficial reflexion upon it, we should be apt to suspect, it was owing to their observing the sun's rising on the
longest day of the year, or summer solstice, and setting their
line by it. For this is supposed to be a method by which they
formerly set our Churches: marking the sun's rising at the
equinox. But the *Druids* were too good astronomers and
mathematicians to need so mean an artifice: nor does it correspond to the quantity precisely enough. Besides, this same
variation appears where it cannot possibly regard the sun's
rising at that

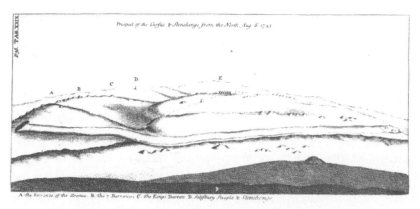

Plate 29. Prospect of the Cursus & Stonehenge from the North Aug. 6, 1723.
A. The Entrance of the Avenue. B. The 7 Barrows. C. The Kings Barrow. D. Salisbury Steeple. E.
Stonehenge.

For, I observ'd the like variation, or very near, in all the other parts relating to this temple before taken notice of; beside the avenue leading up to the temple from the north east, in a strait line; which has the before-mention'd variation all the way. At the bottom of the hill, this avenue divides into two wings, each going off from the list mention'd part, with a decent sweep; the one to the left hand, westward, the other to the right hand, eastward. They go off with a like angle, and that angle varies the like quantity. The western wing goes to the *cursus*, before observ'd, the place upon the downs, half a mile off *Stonehenge*, made for races with chariots and horses. The right hand wing of the avenue runs directly eastward for a mile together, pointing to a place on an angle of the river, called *Radfin*. This part of the avenue, which was intended by the founders, to have been drawn precisely east and west, varies about 5 or 6 degrees to the south.

Likewise, that great work of the *cursus* itself, which stretches its length across the downs, from east to west, like a line of latitude upon the globe, varies such a like quantity, from true east and west, the same way. The meridian line of *Stonehenge* passes exactly through the middle of this *cursus*.

Further, at the east end of this *cursus*, the huge bank of earth, above 200 foot long, made across the end of the *cursus*, as a *meta*, and whereon sat the princes and judges of the prizes: This bank of earth is drawn exactly at a right angle with the *cursus*, consequently due north and south, but with the variation before spoken of. These, and other like observations here, as well as in other *Druid* Works, appear'd to me no otherwise to be accounted for, but that the *Druids* us'd a magnetical compass, in laying down the works: and that the needle vary'd so much, at that time, from the true meridian line.

I remember I open'd this affair, near 20 Years ago, to Dr. *Halley*, who was of the same sentiment. Nor am I the first who suspected the *Phœnicians* of old were possessed of this great secret, as well as the *Chinese*, from times immemorial. I am not moved to think otherwise by what *Bochart* writes against it. The very name of the magnet *lapis Heraclius* strongly suggests, the *Tyrian* navigator before-mention'd knew it, as is well argued by *Fuller* in his Miscellanies, IV. 19. And many things occur, in the mythology of the antients, wherein (if I mistake not) I discern most evident traces of this knowledge of the directive power of the magnet. We are not to despise the fables of the antients, but to make the best use of them, and search out for their latent truths. My predecessor *Cumberland*, observes in *Sanchoniathon*, p. 325. "that *Apollodorus* (for instance) hath many truths in his mythic history, deriv'd from the tradition of *Phœnician*, and *Egyptians*, planting *Athens*." And the *Greeks*, those happy practitioners in writing, as well as other arts, took the unlucky turn of the *marvellous*, to so exorbitant a degree, as to write nothing without it. In *Apollodorus*, put out by the learned Dr. *Gale*, p. 114. we have an account of the 10th labour of *Hercules*, his conquest of *Cadiz*, or *Gadira*, as then call'd, or *Erythea*. We are told, the hero set up the 2 pillars at the Streights mouth, at *Gibralter*, or then *Tartessus*; which we may reasonably suppose some temple made of these rough stones, or some *main ambres*, like those we mention'd before, the *petræ ambrosiæ* in the *Tyrian* coins. Then, "says our author, going on his journey, the rays of the sun were so vehement upon him, that he hid the boldness to draw his bow against him. The god admiring the intrepidity of the man, gave him a golden cup with which he sail'd over the ocean." *Pisander* in his IId. book, (in *Atheneus Deipnos.* XI.) writes the same, only that *Oceanus* lent him the cup. *Panyasis* in his I. of the history of *Hercules*, says, he begg'd it of *Nereus*, son of *Sol*, and with it sail'd to *Erythea*. (Macrob. *Saturn.* XXI. 5.) *Theoclytus*, in *Atheneus* aforesaid, in his II. *de tempest.* mentions the same thing. He said it before in his *Titanomachia*. *Pherecydes*, in his III. of history, quoted both in *Atheneus* and *Macrobius*, tells a story somewhat like that of *Apollodorus*, but more particular. *Servius Æn.* VII, mentions it, but as some of the former, makes the cup of brass, instead of gold. *Alexander Ephesius* the like. All very antient writers. *Lucian* says, that *Hercules* sail'd in a sea-conch shell. What can we understand by all this, mention'd by so many grave authors, but a compass-box, which enabled him to sail the great ocean, and penetrate to our northern island, less obnoxious to the suns vehement heat? Add to this, in the same place, *Apollodorus* speaks of his fighting *Albion* and *Dercynus*, by *Mela*, called *Bergion*, Sons of *Neptune*; which were the most antient names of the *Britannic* Isles, before the name of *Britain*. *Diodorus Siculus*, in his IV. book delivers a like account of this 10th labour of *Hercules*, but in a mere historical manner. And adds, that when he return'd by *Sicily*, he dedicated a grove to *Geryon* the hero, where, to his time, the people did religious rites. For this affair of sacred groves, we know our *Druids* were famous. He built a temple likewise at *Gades*. We are not to suppose it a cover'd edifice, like what posterity call'd a temple, but an open one, according to the mode of those days. Cover'd temples, at that time, being a thing unknown in the world. Afterward, a magnificent temple, properly, was there built to him. *Mela* witnesses, that it was our *Egyptian Hercules*, who was there worshipped. For I suppose our *Egyptian* and the *Tyrian Hercules* to be all one. The same mention'd by the name of *Assis*, in *Manethons* XVII. *Dynasty*, in *Josephus* c. App. in *Africanus, Eusebius*, and *Syncellus. Apollonius* II. 14. writes, it was not the *Theban* but the *Egyptian Hercules* that came to *Gades:* which is confirm'd by *Hecateus*. And *Herodotus*, in *Euterpe* says, *Hercules* is a very antient deity among the *Egyptians*, not so, among the *Greeks*. And I suppose this hero lived at, or very near the time of the patriarch *Abraham*.

These were the times about the beginning of idolatry. And *Hercules* was far from being an idolater himself, though worshipp'd afterwards, for his great exploits, and perhaps on this very account of his inventing or knowing the use of the compass. This is the Hercules kneeling on one knee, a constellation in heaven, taken notice of by *Dionysius Halycarn.* by *Tzetzes, Hyginus, Æschylus* and others. It seems to indicate his piety; for which the astronomers his disciples plac'd him in the heavens. He kneels upon the arctic circle, and supports the zodiac on his shoulders; tho' this is not understood by the painting on our modern globes. The *Phœnicians*, his successors in the tin trade of *Britain*, kept the trade and the very name of the Island as a great secret; as well as the use of the compass, till it was lost with them. But it seems highly probable, because *Lucian* describes *Hercules* with a sphere in his hand, that he affixed the present Asterisms of the zodiac: and his successors, the *Phœnicians*, propagated them.

'Tis next to our present purpose, to consider that famous oracle of *Jupiter Ammon* in *Africa*, to be referr'd to the most early times of idolatry: render'd illustrious by *Alexander* the Great taking a journey to it. Which gives us the opportunity of knowing somewhat of it.

> *Quamvis Æthiopum populis, Arabumq; beatis*
> *Gentibus, ac Indis, unus sit Jupiter Ammon.*   Lucan.

All these nations, with *Egypt* and *Africa*, were peopled by the posterity chiefly of *Ham*. They were the first that fell into idolatry, and worshipped their common progenitor, call'd *Amynus*, in *Sanchoniathon*. *Hecateus* says, *Amoûn*, as the *Egyptians* write it, is the word of those that invoke god, and that they meant somewhat very mysterious by it. The history of its origin is this. *Bacchus*, the hero, or demigod, travelling through the sandy desarts of *Africa*, with a great army, was perishing with thirst; he pray'd to his father *Jupiter* for relief, who sent a *ram* that show'd him a spring, sav'd him and his host. Out of gratitude, the hero builds a temple there, to the deity who thus aided him under the form of a *ram*.

Plate 30. Prospect from the west end of the Cursus of Stonehenge
A. the eastern meta. B. the eastern wing of the avenue. C. Stonehenge.

There is no room to doubt, that this is in part copied from the transaction of the children of *Israel*, in the *Arabian* wilderness. They have added to it, a name and notion borrowed from patriarchal tradition, of a divine person, symboliz'd by a ram; horned, anointed, which is all one. We christians mean *Messiah*. Innumerable passages in old authors, which I might cite, innumerable monuments of antiquity in sculpture, shew, that *Jupiter Ammon* was figur'd as a ram, with a ram's head, with rams horns. They applied the patriarchal notion of the *Messiah*, to their progenitor *Ham*, in an idolatrous way: and deified him under that character. There is a very remarkable passage in *Herodotus*, which, it is worth our while, to transcribe.

In Euterpe cap. 42. that author tells us, why the *Theban Egyptians* pay so great a regard to the sheep. "*Hercules* on his importunity to *Jupiter*, that he might have the honour personally to see him, at length prevail'd. And the god consented to exhibit himself to his view, under this device. *viz. Jupiter* cut off a ram's head, put the skin over his own head, and thus

149

appear'd to *Hercules*. Whence the *Egyptians* made the statue of *Jupiter*, with a ram's head, and call *Jupiter Ammôun*. Whence they hold sheep for sacred animals, never kill them but once a year, upon the festival day of *Jupiter*, when only one ram is sacrificed, and his head put upon the statue of *Jupiter*; all that are there present, beat the ram, and at last he is buried in a sacred urn."

It is impossible not to see, that this is derived from that history recorded, *Exodus* xxxiii. *Moses* desires of *Jehovah* repeatedly, that he might see him. He calls it seeing his glory. He is answer'd at length. "I will make all my *goodness* pass before thee, and I will proclaim the *name* of *Jehovah* before thee. Thou canst not see my face, but I will put thee in a cleft of the rock, and cover thee with my hand, whilst I pass by. Thou shalt see my back parts only." Here he notoriously promises *Moses*, that he shall see him, in a symbolical form. In the next chapter, *Jehovah* descended in the luminous cloud, or *Shechinah*, and proclaimed the name of *Jehovah*; recites those attributes that relate to his dealings with mankind, in the strongest point of light; "his goodness and mercy, and long-suffering, forgiving iniquity, transgression and sin: but adds, he will by no means clear the guilty, but visit the fathers iniquity upon the children." Wherein our original and fatal transgression is sufficiently intimated, and that God's justice is equal to his mercy; and the necessity of a divine redemption by sacrifice, which in scripture language is call'd, "the lamb slain from the foundation of the world."

All this the most ancient nations had a knowledge of, from patriarchal tradition. When they laps'd into idolatry, they applied these good notions to their new idolatry, and made statues from the symbolical and figurative forms of speech, us'd in true religion. Their sacrificing the ram on the festival day of *Jupiter*, their beating the ram, putting his head on the statue of their deity, burying him in a sacred urn: all most evidently pointing out the notions they had, in the most early times, of the suffering statue of the *Messiah*. And such was the origin, in short, of *Jupiter Ammon*. But it appears, by what learned authors write, on *Curtius's* description of his statue, that a magnetical compass box made one considerable part of his sacreds. This we read in *Hyde* Pers. relig. p. 495. in *Curtius* publish'd by *Pitiscus*, and by *Rader* the jesuite, and *Schottus* in *Ortelius*, by *Fuller*, *Herwart* and others. "This compass box with the statue of the deity, was set in a golden ship (the golden cup of *Hercules*) and carried in procession on the shoulders of the priests, accompanied by women singing an hymn in their own language." I doubt not, but the circumstance of carrying this golden ship, on the shoulders of the priests, is an imitation of the *Mosaic* ark in the march of the *Israelites*, thro' the wilderness, during their forty years pilgrimage. Tho' they mistook the reason of the thing; the *Jewish* church then being in a military and travelling state. But where the camp rested, the ark was reposited, in the *adytum* of the tabernacle: so likewise when in possession of the land of *Canaan*. This is sufficient proof, that the *Lybians* herein, copied after the *Israelites*, not *vice versa*, as our moderns are willing to think, in these cases.

*Curtius* tells us, the habit of *Ammon's* statue was made of *Smaragd* and other precious stones, wrought in *Mosaic* work. Which I take to be too, in imitation of the pontifical attire, under *Moses's* administration: particularly of the sacred, oracular pectoral, made of *Mosaic* work, with gems. I apprehend, that beside the statue of *Ammon*, there was a figure of (the upper part at least of) a *ram*, on the compass box: which was the oracle. And it is easy to guess how this may be managed for the purpose; even beyond the trick of *Januarius's* blood, and other *Popish* devices.

151

Hence we may better understand the famous golden fleece, which occasioned the *Argonautic* expedition, one of the earliest and most memorable *Æra's* of the *Grecian* history. If we suppose this golden fleece to be a compass box, we see the reason why the choice youth of *Greece* set out upon that voyage: which, as all other matters of ancient history, among the *Greeks*, is so unaccountably puft up with the leaven of fable. It became navigators to run any hazard for such a treasure. If we enquire into its origin, it is thus. *Phrixus* son of *Athamas* and *Nepheles* (according to the *Greeks*) had a ship given him by his mother. The ship is call'd in the fable a golden *ram*, or the ram with a golden fleece (the same thing as *Hercules's* golden cup.) In this, he and his sister *Helle*, flying the ill-usage of their mother-in-law *Ino*, sail away by sea. *Helle* affrighted in the voyage, falls overboard and gives name to the *Hellespont*. *Phrixus* continues the voyage, and goes to *Æetes* king of *Colchis*, where he hangs up his golden *ram* in the temple, to *Jupiter Phyxius*, (one would be apt to imagine they meant *Pyxius*, alluding to the box.) *Jason* made his far-fam'd expedition thither afterward, and stole it. But the ram was placed in the heavens, among the constellations, as a memorial; the first sign in the *Zodiac:* which shews the high antiquity of the story.

This account manifestly pretends very great antiquity, and some signal event. I observe this *Ino* their mother-in-law, is said to be the nurse of *Bacchus*, and throwing herself with her son *Melicerte* into the sea, became a goddess, under the name of *Leucothea*. Her son became a god, under the name of *Palæmon*. This *Melicerte* is allowed by all the learned, to be no other than our *Melcartus* above-mention'd. *Palæmon* is *Hercules*, says *Hesychius*. *Palæmon* is his name of deification. *Pausanias* in the beginning of his *corinthiaca* informs us, this *apotheosis* of *Ina* and *Melicerta* was the occasion of founding the famous *Isthmian* games. *Plutarch* says the same, and

*Phavorinus.* Again, I observe, *Phrixus* is said to be son of *Nephele* (a cloud) whence call'd *nubigena* by *Columella.* We must hence expect somewhat very secret and obscure. Further, all writers say openly this *ram* or ship of *Phrixus* was oracular and could speak upon occasion. So all the writers of the *Argonautics* too will have the ship *Argos* to be loquacious and oracular. *Magnes* another name of the load-stone is often call'd *Adamas*, which seems to be no other than *Athamas.* *Apollodorus* makes *Magnes* the son of *Æolus*, who marrying *Nais*, inhabited the isle *Seriphus. Æolus* was a great sailor, invented sails, and studied the winds, therefore deified and made the god of the winds. I suppose it all ends in the mysterious invelopement of the knowledge of the magnetic compass.

I hope for the readers candour, in reciting thus much from antient fable, which I did as concisely as possible. But in matters of obscure antiquity, we must make use of all helps. And in heathen antiquity we have no other. A strictly historical way of writing in former times, is only to be expected in the sacred canon of the *Jews*.

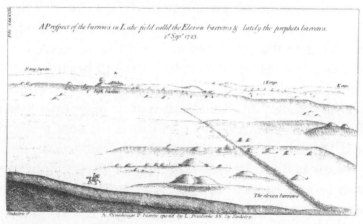

Plate 31. A Prospect of the barrows in Lake field called the Eleven barrows & lately the prophets barrows 2ᵈ. Sepʳ. 1723. A. Stonehenge. P. barrow opened by L. Pembroke. SS by Stukeley.

And what is remarkable, after God's holy spirit had deserted them, their writers became the greatest fablers in the world, and, if possible, out-did the *Greeks*, in that way.

One would imagine, the fashion of these most antient charts, was to divide the circle into 12 parts, and affix the celestial signs of the zodiac to them; beginning with the east at aries, where the sun rises at the equinoxes; and thence they might call the box by the name of *aries*, as shewing the east where *aries* is plac'd. As now the *Turks* and *Arabians* call it *kibla noma, i.e.* shewing the *kibla*, or south point, the way toward which they turn their faces in devotion. So we only enquire for the north point; and call it the lode-stone, because it shews the lode-star or north pole. But 'tis all one; any one point in a circle being found, the red are found too.

From what has been said, it seems probable, that the fable of the hero finding out the spring in the sandy desarts of *Africa*, by the help of a ram sent from *Jupiter*, means the travelling over those immense plains by the help of a compass, which they call'd by the name of a *ram*, or a golden ram. And that the possessors of the antient oracle of *Ammon* had such a secret, which they cunningly applied to the sacreds of their deity. Probably, in that most early age, they had not improv'd the use of it to the pitch and manner that we enjoy, with a needle; and *that* set upon a central pin: but having found out the veracity of the magnet, they put it into a boat, which was to swim on water, and therein it would have liberty to turn itself to its proper direction. And this is the sentiment of the learned Dr. *Wallis*, in the *Philosophical Transactions*, N°. 278. This boat was the better a handle for the mythologists to call *Hercules*'s vessel a golden cup, because cups were made in the shape of a boat, and had the same denomination, *cymbium.*

Those learned commentators upon *Curtius* abovementioned agree, there was a stone along with the statue of *Ammon*, carried about in the golden ship; and perhaps, hence the antient navigators took the hint of applying the figure of the *ram* to their compasses, however form'd, and gave it the name of the *ram*, or golden fleece, which the Greek fables, their most antient history, ring of: and hence their ships deriv'd their oracular quality. *Phrixus*'s ship, the golden *ram*, being said to speak on occasion, as well as the ship *argos*. The stupendous properties of this stone, without difficulty, would persuade even those above the vulgar, that there was a divine principle in it, quite metaphysical, consequently oracular. And in the dawnings of idolatry, the evil agent who was vigilant to pervert every thing to his own purpose, would not fail to make great use of the secrets of the magnet. The intire notion of oracles among the heathen, is caused by the devil's mimickry of God's transactions among the patriarchs and the *Jews*. But I believe the *Egyptians* took their notion of carrying a boat in all their religious processions, from this magnetic boat, of which both *Herodotus* and *Plutarch* inform us. For they intended it to signify the movement and descent of the divine ideas from the supreme mind; especially the very fountain and principal of those ideas: and it must be own'd to be admirably well chose. Hence the top and the bottom of the verge or *limbus* of the celebrated *Iliac* table, is adorn'd with a boat. In one a ram, in the other a bull. Meaning the origin of the chain of ideas flowing from the divine mind. 'Tis highly probable, *that* with the ram is the copy of *Jupiter Ammon*'s boat, mention'd by *Curtius*. And I suppose this is *Herwart*'s opinion, but I have not yet seen his book. Of this I shall discourse larger in my explication of the *Bembin* table. However *Herodotus* tells us in his II. book, that the temple of *Jupiter Ammon* took its rise from *Phœnicia*. I only mention this for the sake of those that are over acting the credit of antiquities in *Egypt*.

We learn in *Plutarch*'s discourse de *Isid. & Osir*, that the ship *argos* of the *Greeks*, was is reality the ship that our *Hercules* sail'd round the world in.

Further, this oracular ship has its name *argos*, says my friend Mr. *Baxter, gloss. ant. rom.* from the *Hebrew* and *Syrian* word *argan*, an ark. Which confirms what I said above, concerning the carrying about the ship of *Ammon* on the shoulders of the priests. *Strabo* in II. of his geography, mentions the temple of *Leucothea*, built by *Phrixus* at *Colchos*; that there was an oracle there; and that the sheep was never slain at the place. This shews its relation to that of *Jupiter Ammon*. *Leucothea* is the name of consecration of *Hercules* his mother, *Hercules* himself being call'd *Palæmon*; both made sea deities: from the extraordinary fame of *Hercules*, the first and great sea captain. *Pausanias* in *Atticis* says, he was buried in the Corinthian *Isthmus*; where the *Isthmian* games were kept to his memory. But *Mela* writes, that his remains were at *Gades*. It's probable there was only an honorary monument of him at the *Isthmus*, as founder: as the honorary monument of *Jolaus* mention'd to be among the *Thebans*, by the *Stadium*, p. 42.

Mr. *Baxter* in *gloss. ant. rom. ascania* makes *Phrixus* to be *Aphricus*, and the same person as *Jupiter Ammon*, or the founder of the temple of *Jupiter Ammon*; rather, of that prior to *Jupiter Ammon*. We are not to regard the little artifices of the *Greeks*, who draw all celebrated events and persons of antiquity, into their own country. *Aphricus*, no doubt, is the *Aphre* before-mentioned, son of *Midian*, son of *Abraham*; whom *Cleodemus* makes an associate of *Hercules*, in his *Lybian* wars. *Josephus* makes him the conqueror of *Lybia*, and that he gave name to *Africa*. 'Tis not unlikely but that he is the hero that travell'd over these barren lands by the help of the compass, as his countrymen the *Arabians* have from times immemorial practised, in travelling over their own desarts. And might probably erect a patriarchal temple there; and in times of his posterity it degenerated into the idolatrous temple of *Jupiter Ammon:* And there the compass box of the hero remain'd, and was converted into part of the heathen sacreds.

'Tis no very strange matter, is they at another time call this same hero *Bacchus,* therein confounding him with the like travels of the *Israelites,* through the *Arabian* desarts. We are not to expect these histories of old times involv'd in fable, absolutely consistent. But is this account be agreeable to truth or near it; then we may imagine the same *Aphre,* by the *Greeks* call'd *Phrixus,* according to Mr. *Baxter,* pass'd the *Hellespont,* made the expedition into *Colchis,* and built a like temple there. And a compass box called the golden *ram,* was made alike part of the object of their adoration. This is exceedingly confirm'd by the report of *Herodotus* and *Diodorus S.* who say, the *Colchi* practised the rite of circumcision, a matter which the learned cannot account for; but appears plain from hence: these being the descendants of *Abraham.* They say, at the same time, that the *Ethiopians* practise the like: and that 'tis no recent custom among them, but from the beginning. I apprehend by *Ethiopians* are meant *Arabians,* who are people descended from *Abraham. Herodotus* says likewise the *Egyptians* circumcis'd, which must be accounted for in this same manner; some *Arabian* or *Ethiopian* nation bringing the custom among them. As a further confirmation of *Phrixus* being *Aphricus, Bochart* shews the *Colchic* and *Hebrew* tongue is much a-kin. And thus we may account for what Mr. *Toland,* p. 133. says, that the idiom of the *Irish* language (which we suppose the remnant of the most antient oriental,) has a mixture of *Arabic* in it.

I saw a book in Dr. *Mead's* library, *Museo de las medallas desconecidas Espanolas,* p. 35. No. 82, 83. are two ancient unknown medals, such as they often find in *Spain*. The first a head (not of the best workmanship) on the obverse, young, but heroical enough, a necklace on. Behind it A Φ P A in the old *Phœnician* character, like the *Samaritan*. Reverse a horseman, and under the exergue another word in like *Punic* character. The other Nº. 83. has the same head in the obverse, but without the necklace: and A Φ P A before, in plain *Greek*, behind a dolphin. The reverse as the last. There is another such coin in the same book, no difference,

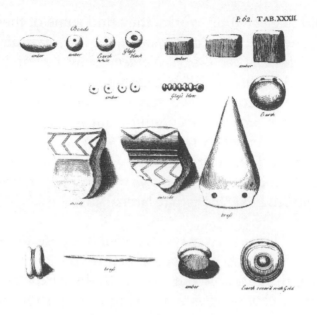

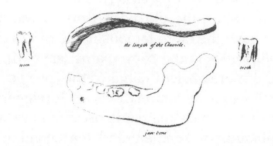

Plate 32. Female Celtic ornaments found in a barrow north of Stonehenge which I open'd 5 July 1723. among burnt bones, all drawn as big as Life.

but the name and dolphin transpos'd: I verily believe this is our *Aphra*, or *Apher* in our *English* translation call'd *Epher*, *Gen.* xxv. 4. struck by some city in *Spain*, who acknowledged him their founder.

It is remarkable enough, what Mr. *Norden* writes, in his history of *Cornwall*. The *Cornish* men universally suppose that the *Jews* are the people who first work't in their rocks, for tin:

and in old neglected tin-works, they find some of their tools. The workmen call them *attal sarazin*, the *Jews* cast off works, in their *Hebrew* speech, says *Norden*. Now I apprehend he means our *Arabians*: and it is a circumstance confirming the former notions. And to it we may refer the origin of the odd reports, of our *Stonehenge* coming from *Africa* and the like. By the *Greeks*, *Hercules Melcartus* or *Melicerta*, and *Phryxus* or *Apricus* are made half brothers: by *Josephus*, *Hercules* is son-in-law to *Aphricus*. The *Phœnicians* paid tythe. So the *Arabians*, in *Pliny*, the like: being patriarchal customs.

*Aphricus* or *Phryxus* we may very well suppose to be father of the *Phrygians*. And his expedition thro' the *propontis* to the *Euxine* sea, the *Greeks* colour over with their *Helle* and *Hellespont*. But we cannot entertain too high a respect for him, because I see it no less reasonable, to refer the origin of the *Britons* to him. I mean that eastern colony that came hither with *Hercules*, upon the old possessors or *aborigines Albionites*, which gave the more famous name of *Britain* to the island. The *Brigantes* is the same name, says Mr. *Baxter* the common and more ancient name of this people: who being driven northwards by inundations of foreigners from the continent in after times, the name became more appropriate to the inhabitants of *Yorkshire* and the neighbouring counties. In *Tacitus* the *Brigantes* are called *maxima Brittanorum natio*. At the same time they forc'd the ancientest possessors, the *Albionites* or *Albanians* still more northwards. Likewise many of these *Brigantes* pass'd into *Ireland*, where they became a famous nation. The *Bryges*, *Phryges*, *Phrixi*, *Brisones*, *Brigantes*, *Britons* are intirely synonimous words in different dialects. And this assignment of the origin of our ancestors, very well accounts for that notion of their *Phrygian* or *Trojan* descent, so riveted in the minds of the old *Britons*. A notion which prevail'd among some of the *Gallic* nations on the continent, and they had retain'd the memory of it, in the time of

*Ammianus Marcellinus,* who mentions it. Likewise in *Cæsar's* time, some *Gallic* nations, claimed kindred with the *Romans*; probably upon this very account.

This is, in short, some presumptive evidence we have, of *Hercules* and *Aphricus* planting *Britain,* introducing the Druids with the patriarchal religion: and concerning the knowledge they had of the use of the compass. This whole matter will be further considered, when I come to treat of it expressly. At present we will continue the history of the compass, as it became more fully known to the world.

*Martinius* in his *Atlas,* and *Gilbertus de magnete, Lib.* I. 2. show us, the *Chinese* have us'd the magnetic needle from times immemorial: that they have a trick of telling fortunes with it: as the heathen afore-mentioned made it oracular. The *Arabians* likewise have us'd it, for travelling over the great and wild desarts, of weeks together, where there is no track to guide them; nor have they any notion of time when they began this practice. *Herwartius* published *admiranda ethnicæ theologiæ,* wherein he endeavours to prove that the old *Egyptians* had the use of the magnetic needle, and that the *Bembin* table contains the doctrine of it, invelop'd in hieroglyphicks. The learned *Fuller* in his *Miscellanies Lib.* 4. 19. asserts, that the *Phœnicians* knew the use of it, which they endeavour'd to conceal by all possible means, as they did their trading in general. That it was lost with them, as many other arts, their *ars plumaria,* the dying of purple, (the invention of our *Hercules* of *Tyre*) the *Hebrew* poetry, and other curious knowledge, which is perished.

'Tis not unlikely that the lodestone being applied to religious use, was one cause of its being forgot: together with the secrecy of the *Phœnician* voyages. *Suetonius* in *Nero,* speaks of a prophetic needle, which the emperor us'd to pay his devotions to. The learned *Burman* shews, that most, or all of the old MSS. and printed books, read it *acuncula, acucula,* or *acungula;* which, in my opinion, the criticks have causelesly corrected into *icuncula:* because they had no notion of the magnetic needle being understood by it.

Monsieur *Fauchet,* a famous *French* antiquary, in his antiquities of *France,* quotes some verses from a poet in that country, who wrote A.D. 1180. wherein is as plain a description of the mariner's box, as words can make. The poet mentions it by accident, not as a thing new and strange. *Osorius* in his discourse of the acts of king *Emanuel,* refers the use of the compass among the *Europeans,* to *Gama* and the *Portuguese,* who found it among some barbarous pyrates, about the *Cape* of *Good Hope;* who probably were some remains of the old *Phœnicians,* or *Arabians,* or at least have preserved from them, this practice. About A.D. 1260. *Paulus Venetus* is said to have brought it from *China;* by the great author on the magnet, our countryman *Gilbert. Genebrand* in his *chron.* says, the use of the lode-stone reviv'd among us about A.D. 1303. by *Fl. Melvius* a *Neapolitan,* and others attribute it about that time to *John Goia* a *Neapolitan. Joseph de Costa* says, some *Mahometan* seamen whom *Vasquez de Gama* met with near *Mosambick,* who had sail'd those seas by the use thereof, taught it him. I observe our ancient *Britons,* the *Welsh,* call a steersman or pilot *llywydd,* whence no doubt comes our *English* word lode-stone, and lode-star, the north-pole. *Llyw* is the helm of a ship in *British. Lodemanage* in *Skinner's etymology* an old *English* word, signifying the price paid to the pilot. Our lords of the *Cinque Ports* keep a court at *Dover,* by that name. These things seem to indicate some memorial of the magnet left among the *Welsh,* from the oldest times: and of its application to sailing.

Thus have we given a kind of history of this prodigy in nature, the magnetic needle: to confirm our suspicion, that the *British* Druids knew the use of it, and used it in these works of theirs, which we have been treating of. We learn in the *Philosophical Transactions, Lowthorp*, Vol. II. p. 601. that there are considerable veins of the magnet, in our own country, in *Devonshire*; where the *Phœnicians* and Druids must needs be very conversant.

We return now to our first subject *Stonehenge*, and apply what has been said, to the observation we there made. It is not to be thought, that the Druids, men who employed themselves in those noble studies, which *Cæsar* gives us an account of; and who were at the pains of bringing these vast stones together, from such a considerable distance of 16 miles: I say, it is not to be thought, but that they would be nice and exact in placing them. And this, not only particularly, in respect of each other, upon the projected ground-plot: but also in general, in respect of the quarters of the heavens. And this I found to be a just surmise, when I examined their works for several years together, with sufficient accuracy, with a *theodilite*. As I took notice before, the works of one place regarded the cardinal points, but with a certain uniform variation therefrom. Whence I grounded my conjecture, that they were set by a compass, which at that time varied, according to that quantity observ'd. Of which property of variation we may well suppose, the Druids were ignorant. This I now propose for the rule of investigation, of the time when *Stonehenge* was erected. Hoping the reader will judge as favourably of the attempt, as things of this great antiquity require.

The variation at *Stonehenge* is about 6 or 7 degrees, from the north eastward. I have in order to form our hypothesis, set down a scheme of the state of the variation in *England*, from the best observations I could meet with Dr. *Halley* takes notice, that the variation at *Paris* is always 2 degrees and a half more easterly than with us. *Orontius Finæus* in 1550 observ'd it to be there, about 9 degrees, easterly, therefore to reduce it, I have stated it at 11 degrees 30 and from thence continued it,

Plate 33. Prospect from Bushbarrow.
a. Runway hill. b. Oldbury. D. Stonehenge.

to the present time, as in the ensuing table.

| *Anno Dom.* | Observation. | Variation. |
|---|---|---|
| | | deg. min. |
| 1550 | By *Finæus* | 11 30 east. |
| 1580 | Mr. *Burroughs* | 11 15 east. |
| 1600 | | 8 0 east. |
| 1622 | Mr. *Gunter* | 6 0 east. |
| 1634 | Mr. *Gellibrand* | 4 5 east. |
| 1642 | | 3 5 east. |
| 1657 | Mr. *Bond* | 0 0 |
| 1665 | Mr. *Bond* | 1 22 west. |
| 1666 | Capt. *Sturmy* | 1 27 west. |
| 1667 | Capt. *Sturmy* | 1 33 weft. |

| | | |
|---|---|---|
| 1672 | Dr. *Halley* | 2 30 west. |
| 1683 | | 4 30 west. |
| 1685 | | 5  5 west. |
| 1692 | | 6  0 west. |
| 1723 | | 11  0 west. |
| 1733 | | 12  0 west. |
| 1740 | | 15 45 west. |

By this table it appears, that in the space of 180 years, the variation of the magnetic needle in *England,* has shifted from 11 degrees and a half eastward, to 11 degrees and a half westward. In 90 years the medium of those extremes, which was 1657, there was no variation at all; the needle pointing due north and south. But alas our observations extend no farther. We know not the bound of the variation, on either hand: nor the quantity of its motion, when thereabouts. Mr. *Geo. Graham* thinks it is now near the western bound. It is very slow, in all probability, when upon the return, and as it were, stationary: like the sun's motion at the tropics, when it is returning. So that the nice determination of its circle, and of its motion, is reserved for remote posterity. Dr. Halley conjectures, that the whole period of variation, is perform'd in about 700 years. Upon this supposition, in gross, we may thus found our conjecture, of the time of building of *Stonehenge.*

By what we can find, the variation is about 9 minutes in a year, or a degree and a half in to years, at this part of its circle. Now I observ'd at *Stonehenge,* that the eastern wing of the avenue, the *cursus* and other parts belonging to the temple, abated somewhat in their variation, eastward, being somewhat less than that of the temple itself. It is highly reasonable to believe, that the great work of *Stonehenge* could not take less than half a score years in building: and that those other works were made in succeeding years, not long after it was finished. From hence I gather, which way the magnetic variation was moving, at the time of sounding *Stonehenge, viz.* from east toward no variation and so to west. This must be the foundation of our *calculus*.

Therefore at the time of the founding of *Stonehenge*, the variation was about the same quantity and place, as about A.D. 1620. in our preceeding table. Supposing with Dr. *Halley*, the revolution of this variation be about 700 years, three intire revolutions thereof, bring us to about the year of the city of *Rome* 280. which is about 460 years before our Saviour's time: 420 years before *Cæsar* invaded *Britain*. About 100 years before our Saviour's birth, *Divitiacus* made the *Wansdike* north of *Stonehenge*, and drove the possessors of this fine country of the *Wiltshire* downs, northwards. So that the Druids enjoyed their magnificent work of *Stonehenge*, but about 360 years. And the very great number of barrows about it, requires, that we should not much shorten the time. Sir *Isaac Newton* in his *Chronology*, reckons 19 years for a medium of a king's reign. So that in that space, there were about 19 kings, in this country. And there seems to be about that number of royal barrows (in my way of conjecturing) about the place.

I observe, this time we have assign'd for the building of *Stonehenge*, is not long after *Cambyses's* invasion of *Egypt*. When he committed such horrid outrages there, and made such dismal havock, with the priests and inhabitants in general, that they fled the country to all parts of the world. Some went as far as the *East Indies*, and there taught many of the antient *Egyptian* customs; as is taken notice of by the learned. It is not to be doubted that some of them fled as far westward, into the island of Britain, and introduced some of their learning, arts and religion, among the Druids; and perhaps had a hand in this very work of *Stonehenge:* the only one that I know of, where the stones are chizel'd. All other works of theirs, are of rude stones, untouch'd of tool, exactly after the patriarchal and *Jewish* mode: therefore older.

This was at a time, when the *Phœnician* trade was at height, the readier a conveyance to *Britain:* it was before the second temple at *Jerusalem* was built: before the *Grecians* had any history.

END

Plate 34. Carvilii Regis Tumulus Iuly 29 1723.
Sorbiodunum. C. Salisbury. D. the Icening street road. F. Harnham hill.

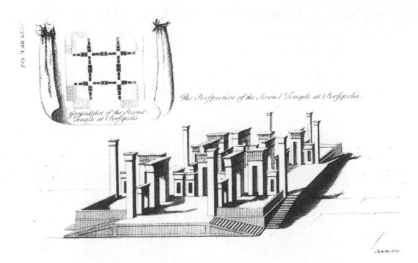

Plate 35. The Perspective of the Second Temple at Persepolis.
(inset) Groundplot of the Second Temple at Persepolis.

# More Books from Cornerstone

## Masonic Enlightenment
The Philosophy, History and Wisdom of Freemasonry
Edited by Michael R. Poll
6x9 Softcover 180 pages
ISBN 1-887560-75-0

## God's Soldiers: Roman Catholicism and Freemasonry
by Dudley Wright
6x9 Softcover 96 pages
ISBN 1-887560-71-8

## Off in a Dream
A collection of poetry and prose
by Aubrey Damhnait Fae
6x9 Softcover 96 pages
ISBN 1-887560-72-6

## A Ghost of a Chance
by Evelyn Klebert
6x9 Softcover 96 pages
ISBN 1-887560-50-5

## The Rosicrucians: Their Rites and Mysteries
by Hargrave Jennings
Michael R. Poll, Editor
Large Format, 8.25 x 11 Softcover 276 pages
ISBN 1-887560-88-2

## Ancient and Modern Initiation
by Max Heindel
6x9 Softcover 96 pages
ISBN 1-887560-18-1

Cornerstone Book Publishers
www.cornerstonepublishers.com

Printed in Great Britain
by Amazon.co.uk, Ltd.,
Marston Gate.